Table of contents

Chapter 1: Introduction	1
Background on Jimmy Savile's rise as a popular television personality in Britain	3
Overview of his reputation as a national treasure and subsequent infamy as a pedophile	5
Introduction to the speculation and exploration of Savile's potential involvement in occult practices	7
Chapter 2: The Seventh Son	9
Examination of Jimmy Savile's birth on October 31, 1926, as the seventh son	11
Discussion on the traditional association of the seventh son with magical powers	13
Speculation on the possible influence of this birth order on Savile's actions and motivations	15
Chapter 3: Connections and Influences	17
Exploration of Savile's relationships with influential people from various fields	19
Analysis of his association with prominent figures and organizations	21
Examination of his honors and knighthoods and their potential significance in occult circles	23
Chapter 4: Language and Symbols	25
Discussion on the potential sinister or occultist use of language by Jimmy Savile	27
Analysis of his intricate use of phrases and symbols, such as "jingle jangle"	29
Examination of the ancient and occult power of language and words, especially when repeated	30
Chapter 5: Alastair Crowley and Thelema	33
Comparison of Jimmy Savile's actions and beliefs with those of Alastair Crowley, a notorious English occultist wizard	35
Exploration of the connections between Savile and the Thelema religion	37
Analysis of the influence of Alastair Crowley's Thelema religion on 1960s bands such as The Beatles	39
Chapter 6: Connections with The Beatles	41
Exploration of Jimmy Savile's extensive relationships with The Beatles	43
Discussion on the potential long-term impact of Jimmy Savile's occult influences on the UK pop music industry	45
Analysis of the similarities between Savile and Count Dracula as "energy vampires"	47
Chapter 7: Secret Societies and Royalty	49
Exploration of Jimmy Savile's potential affiliations with secret societies	51
Analysis of the connections between secret services, royalty, and occult practices in history	53
Examination of Prince Charles' ambiguous gift and note to Savile and its potential significance	55
Chapter 8: The Dualistic Nature of Magic	57
Discussion on the Two Sides of Magic	59
Analysis of his potential involvement in both benevolent and malevolent practices	61
Exploration of the motivations behind his actions and the expanse of his influence	63
Chapter 9: Charitable Work and Manipulation	67
Examination of Jimmy Savile's charitable work and its potential hidden motives	69
Analysis of how his charity work may have served as a means to balance karma and gain access to influential figures	71
Discussion on the concept of gathering "soul energy" through public persona and philanthropy	73
Chapter 10: Ley Lines and Manipulation of Subtle Forces	75
Exploration of the suspected use of ley line locations by Savile for manipulation of subtle energies	77
Analysis of specific locations associated with Savile, such as Stoke Mandeville, Broadmoor, Duncroft, and Broadcasting House	79
Discussion on the potential impact of ley lines in occult practices and personal/societal control	81
Chapter 11: Unravelling the Mystery	83
Questions surrounding Jimmy Savile's alleged power, motivations, and the expanse of his influence	85
Examination of the uncertainty surrounding his backstory and potential secret spy or "fixer" role during the war	87
Analysis of the known connections between secret services, occult practices, and influential figures	89
Chapter 12: Conclusion	91
Summary of the Various Theories and Connections Explored	93
Final Thoughts and Suggestions for Further Exploration	95
Suggestion for Further Research and Investigation	97

Chapter 1: Introduction

In this opening chapter, we embark on a journey into the enigmatic world of Jimmy Savile, a man who once stood as a beloved national treasure of Britain, only to be unmasked as one of the country's most infamous and reviled pedophiles. However, our quest goes beyond the surface-level revulsion caused by his heinous crimes, as we delve into the shadowy realm of speculation and exploration – investigating the possibility of Savile's involvement in occult practices and his use of influence and power to manipulate and control others.

To comprehend the gravity of our inquiry, it is crucial to understand the meteoric rise of Savile as an iconic television personality. A charismatic force that charmed his way into the hearts of millions, his presence on the screen was unparalleled, captivating audiences with his smooth demeanor, flamboyant attire, and larger-than-life persona. From hosting the iconic Top of the Pops to gracing the sacred couch of the esteemed talk show host, he navigated effortlessly through the realm of entertainment, becoming a household name and a trusted figure in every living room across the nation.

But as is often the case, those who shine the brightest cast the darkest shadows. The revelation of Savile's horrendous crimes sent shockwaves through society, leaving a nation grappling with the truth behind the facade. Yet, intriguingly, there are whispers that his malevolent deeds were not simply the twisted actions of one man but potentially part of a far larger, more sinister tapestry – one woven with threads of occult intrigue.

Our journey commences by traversing Savile's early years, delving into his birth on the ominous date of October 31, 1926, a date forever associated with the ancient pagan festival of Samhain. It is here that the arcane nature of our protagonist's story first takes shape, for he entered the world as the seventh son, a position traditionally enveloped in mysticism and tied to the notion of magical powers. Through this lens, we begin to question whether there may have been hidden forces at play even from the very beginning of Savile's existence.

Moving forward, we shall explore the connections and influences that permeated Savile's life, examining the web he spun as he amassed relationships with influential figures from diverse fields. From politicians to royalty, from musicians to fellow television personalities, Savile had an uncanny ability to captivate, drawing people from all walks of life into his sphere of influence. Such a wide-reaching network raises suspicions, hinting at a darker purpose behind his connections – a purpose that may have originated from his alleged involvement in occult circles.

As we continue delving deeper, we shall scrutinize the significance of Savile's honors and knighthoods. For he was not merely a television icon but held prestigious titles within the world of secret societies. A Knight of Malta, a Knight Commander of St. Gregory, and a Knight of the Realm, these accolades carry peculiar connotations, suggesting a possible entanglement in hidden agendas and clandestine practices.

Our exploration will also draw attention to Savile's meticulous use of language and symbols, unraveling the intricate layers of meaning hidden within his public persona. From his distinctive catchphrases, such as the notorious "jingle jangle," to the choice of specific symbols in his attire and actions, we shall decipher the potential occult significance encoded within his words and gestures. By understanding the ancient and occult power of language and symbols, especially when repeated or employed by those vested with influence, we uncover the manipulative tactics employed by Savile to mesmerize and control his unsuspecting victims.

Furthermore, we shall draw compelling parallels between Savile and the notorious English occultist Alastair Crowley, whose infamy precedes him. We explore the shared beliefs and connections, particularly their alleged associations or sympathies with the Thelema religion and the utilization of occult symbols. Intriguingly, we shall also examine the potential influence that Thelema had on the 1960s music phenomenon, with Savile's presiding presence over that era's iconic bands, most notably The Beatles, leading us to question whether occult forces seeped into the backdrop of popular culture itself.

This chapter serves as an introduction to the dark arts of Jimmy Savile, enticing readers to consider the possibility that beneath his charming persona lurked a much more sinister reality. As we peel back the layers of his life, we begin to witness the emergence of a complex web woven with occult influences, secret society affiliations, and signs of ritualistic practices. The ensuing chapters shall further unravel these mysteries, leaving us to grapple with profound questions regarding the intentions and motivations behind Savile's actions and the true extent of his nefarious influence.

Background on Jimmy Savile's rise as a popular television personality in Britain

To understand the enigmatic figure that is Jimmy Savile, it is essential to delve into the depths of his meteoric rise as a beloved television personality in Britain. Born in Leeds, England, on October 31, 1926, he would go on to leave an indelible mark on the nation's collective consciousness.

Savile's entrance into the realm of entertainment can be traced back to his early endeavors in the world of disc jockeying. He possessed an innate ability to connect with audiences through the airwaves, captivating listeners with his magnetic charisma, distinctive voice, and encyclopedic knowledge of music. His radio career took flight during the 1950s when he joined Radio Luxembourg, the influential commercial broadcaster that beamed its signal across the United Kingdom and Europe. It was here that Savile's unique style, coupled with his unparalleled charisma, struck a chord with the British audience.

However, it was in the realm of television that Savile truly came into his own, commanding the small screen with a presence that was at once mesmerizing and enigmatic. In 1964, he became one of the "Originals" on BBC's iconic music program "Top of the Pops," a show that showcased the latest hits and catapulted emerging stars to fame. With Savile at the helm, the show became a cultural phenomenon, eagerly anticipated by millions of viewers each week. His larger-than-life personality, combined with his distinctive dress sense, which often featured flamboyant outfits adorned with extravagant jewelry, became his trademark.

Building upon his success, Savile swiftly ascended the ranks of television stardom, swiftly becoming a household name across the United Kingdom. He became a fixture on various programs, hosting a range of shows that spanned genres and showcased his versatility as a presenter. From the cherished children's program "Jim'll Fix It," in which he would grant the wishes of young viewers, to the long-running chat show "Jim'll Fix It with Salt and Pepper," where he entertained a diverse range of guests with his charismatic banter, Savile conquered every television format he ventured into.

What set Savile apart was his unparalleled ability to connect with people from all walks of life. He had an uncanny knack for making individuals feel special, regardless of their background or social standing. From rubbing shoulders with politicians, royalty, and celebrities to sharing heartfelt moments with everyday people, Savile had a remarkable talent for forging connections, leaving an indelible mark on those he encountered.

Beyond his captivating on-screen presence, Savile's influence extended far beyond the realm of entertainment. He was an avid philanthropist, dedicating significant amounts of time and resources to charitable causes. Savile's charity work garnered widespread recognition, earning him the accolade of being one of the most prolific fundraisers in British history. The proceeds from his endeavors, which included marathon running, supporting hospitals, and fostering relationships with charitable organizations, amounted to millions of pounds.

This extensive charity work, along with his flamboyant public persona, endeared Savile to the British public. He embodied a larger-than-life figure who seemingly possessed an unlimited reserve of kindness and generosity. His charismatic public image only served to deepen the mystery surrounding his true character.

It is this unique combination of captivating charisma, philanthropy, and an encyclopedic knowledge of music that propelled Jimmy Savile to the pinnacle of television stardom in Britain. However, as we delve further into his life and legacy, we shall encounter unsettling questions and revelations that paint a different picture—an exploration into the potential darker undercurrents and occult aspects of Savile's rise to fame and the true motivations behind his actions.

Overview of his reputation as a national treasure and subsequent infamy as a pedophile

Jimmy Savile's reputation as a national treasure of Britain was, for many years, untarnished. His influential presence on television screens and his unwavering commitment to charitable work elevated him to a status of adoration and respect among the British public. However, the subsequent revelation of his horrifying actions shattered this once-idyllic perception, casting a dark and sinister shadow over his legacy.

For decades, Savile was regarded as a figure of exceptional generosity, embodying the qualities of a benevolent and caring individual. His tireless efforts to raise funds for various charitable causes and his unwavering commitment to hospitals and institutions across the country earned him the nickname "Sir Jimmy," further cementing his position as a national treasure. The public held him in high esteem, viewing him as an icon of compassion, charity, and selflessness.

Savile's connection with hospitals played a significant role in crafting his revered image. He was deeply involved with institutions such as Stoke Mandeville Hospital in Buckinghamshire and Broadmoor Hospital in Berkshire, dedicating countless hours and resources to the betterment of the patients. His voluntary work and fundraising efforts endeared him not only to the staff but to the patients themselves, who saw him as a ray of hope and kindness during their most challenging times.

Savile's influence extended beyond his charity work and into the realm of public entertainment. He hosted countless events, both high-profile and grassroots, using his position as a popular television personality to engage and captivate audiences. His televised fundraisers, such as the annual "Jim'll Fix It" appeal, attracted widespread attention and enthusiastic support from viewers, who saw him as a beloved figure using his fame to champion causes close to their hearts.

However, it wasn't until after his death in 2011, at the age of 84, that the reprehensible truth about Savile's dark side emerged, turning his once-glowing reputation on its head. What unraveled was a chilling narrative of sexual abuse, manipulation, and the exploitation of vulnerable individuals, particularly children and young adults.

The revelations shocked the nation and sent shockwaves across the world. As countless victims came forward with accusations, it became apparent that Savile had knowingly used his position of influence, power, and celebrity to prey on the innocent. The magnitude of the abuse was difficult to comprehend, as allegations spanned decades and involved various institutions ranging from hospitals and television studios to charitable organizations.

What followed was a seismic shift in public opinion. The man once regarded as a national treasure was now seen as the epitome of evil. The adoration and respect that had defined Savile's public persona were replaced with anger, outrage, and disbelief. The revelations of his crimes prompted a profound reevaluation of his life and actions, as well as a collective mourning for those who had suffered in silence.

The subsequent investigations and inquiries into Savile's activities revealed a systematic pattern of abuse that had remained hidden for years. His influential connections and the culture of silence surrounding his actions allowed him to escape scrutiny, shielding him from the consequences that should have followed his first transgressions. Institutions that should have protected the vulnerable failed in their duty, allowing Savile to continue his destructive behavior for far too long.

The shocking revelation of Savile's pedophilic activities exposed a stark contrast between his public image and his true nature, leaving the British public grappling with feelings of betrayal, anger, and a pervasive sense of guilt. Questions arose regarding how such flagrant abuse had gone unnoticed for so long, and how a figure so seemingly devoted to charity could harbor such darkness within.

This dramatic shift from national treasure to infamous pedophile sparked a wider conversation about the prevalence of abuse, the importance of listening to victims, and the need for systemic change to prevent such heinous crimes from occurring again. The aftermath of the revelations surrounding Savile's crimes was a painful awakening for the nation, shaking the very foundations of trust and forcing society to confront the realization that evil can often hide behind a captivating facade.

The juxtaposition of Savile's once-revered status with the sickening truth of his actions serves as a stark reminder that appearances can be deceiving, that monsters can often hide in plain sight. The impact of his crimes reverberates to this day, forever tarnishing his legacy and leaving a scar on the collective consciousness of a nation that grapples with the devastating consequences of his abuse.

Introduction to the speculation and exploration of Savile's potential involvement in occult practices

As we venture further into the depths of Jimmy Savile's life, the convoluted mysteries surrounding his reputation and actions lead us to question the potential involvement of occult practices. While the mere mention of the occult conjures images of esoteric rituals, hidden symbols, and clandestine gatherings, it is crucial to approach this subject matter with an open mind, recognizing that the realm of the occult is vast and complex, encompassing a range of beliefs and practices.

The exploration of Savile's alleged connection to the occult is not an attempt to sensationalize or demonize, but rather a diligent examination of the various facets of his life, actions, and associations. It is an endeavor to shed light on the possible motivations that may have fueled his enigmatic persona and darker undertakings.

The occult encompasses a wide spectrum of beliefs and practices steeped in mystery, symbolism, and the pursuit of hidden knowledge. It has fascinated and captivated individuals for centuries, with its allure lying in the potential for accessing extraordinary powers, transcending conventional boundaries, and gaining control over the forces that govern existence.

Within this chapter, we shall embark on an exploratory journey, scrutinizing the threads that connect Savile to the occult. We shall peel back the layers of his life, examining the potential significance of occult beliefs and practices in shaping his actions and motivations.

To delve into this realm, it is crucial to understand that the occult, in its broadest sense, encompasses far more than what is typically perceived as witchcraft, black magic, or devil worship. It encompasses a tapestry of beliefs including astrology, alchemy, divination, ritual magic, mysticism, and esoteric philosophies. These belief systems, often shrouded in secrecy and steeped in symbolism, have long exerted a powerful allure on those seeking answers and hidden truths beyond the mundane.

Within the context of Savile's life, we explore the possibility of his involvement in secret societies and the manipulation of arcane knowledge, tapping into realms beyond the comprehension of the average person. Such organizations, with their hidden agendas and enigmatic rituals, have been present throughout history, exerting invisible influence on various aspects of society. We consider whether Savile was privy to esoteric knowledge and if he used this knowledge as a means of exerting control, manipulating others, or even as a source of power itself.

Furthermore, the numerous connections Savile established with influential figures across politics, entertainment, and royalty raise intriguing questions. Could these associations have facilitated his alleged occult affiliations? Or were they mere coincidences, devoid of any deeper significance? We analyze the interplay between his connections, his public image, and the potential influence exerted by occult circles.

In examining Savile's language, symbols, and actions, we explore the possibility of coded messages, hidden meanings, and ritualistic undertones. We investigate the power of language and how repeated phrases or particular choice of words can have ritualistic and symbolic significance, potentially weaving a web of influence and control. By unraveling these linguistic patterns, we aim to shed light on the potential use of magical language and signs that may have played a role in Savile's enigmatic character.

It is important to note that this exploration into the occult dimensions of Savile's life is not meant to espouse outlandish theories or make sweeping generalizations. Instead, it seeks to uncover potential connections and motivations that go beyond the surface-level understanding of his actions and public persona. By examining the occult implications, we aim to provide a more nuanced understanding of the enigma that was Jimmy Savile and the multifaceted forces that could have shaped his life and legacy.

Chapter 2: The Seventh Son

In this chapter, we embark on a profound exploration of Jimmy Savile's birth on October 31, 1926, as the seventh son, unveiling the intriguing associations tied to this significant aspect of his life. Throughout history and across cultures, the seventh son has been enveloped in an aura of mysticism and has often been attributed with extraordinary powers. We delve into the realm of folklore, mythology, and ancient beliefs to unravel the potential impact of this birth order on Savile's actions and motivations.

The number seven holds a time-honored place in human consciousness, intertwined with notions of luck, divinity, and enchantment. In religious texts and mythologies, it frequently appears in significant contexts, symbolizing completion, harmony, and spiritual awakening. Its echoes resonate within the realms of numerology, astrology, and occult practices, hinting at a deeper significance underlying Savile's enigmatic journey.

Firstly, we must explore the ancient beliefs surrounding the power bestowed upon the seventh child, particularly the seventh son. In many cultures, there are references to the septimus as a blessed or gifted individual possessing supernatural abilities or a unique connection to higher realms. Folklore across Europe, for instance, often speaks of the seventh son of a seventh son being destined for greatness, with exceptional healing capabilities or the potential to become a seer or sage.

Such beliefs, steeped in ancient mystical traditions, invite us to pause and contemplate the potential impact this birth order may have had on Savile's life. Did the cosmic alignment of his birth hold deeper secrets? Could he have carried within him a hidden energy, compelling him towards a path intertwined with esoteric knowledge and occult practices?

Examining the life and actions of Jimmy Savile, it is intriguing to consider the possibility that such mystical associations were not purely coincidental. His charismatic demeanor, his uncanny ability to captivate and influence others, and his mysterious connections to influential figures from various realms of society allude to a man uniquely positioned to harness and manipulate unseen forces.

We delve further into the symbolism attributed to the number seven, as it pertains to Savile's life. Across numerous belief systems, the seventh son is often deemed to possess innate gifts or talents, ranging from the ability to commune with spirits to uncovering secrets hidden from ordinary mortals. Were these potential attributes reflected in Savile's actions, his extraordinary charisma and ability to gain the trust of others? Or did they manifest in more clandestine practices, leading him down a path that strayed far from the public image he carefully cultivated?

Additionally, we explore the historical significance of October 31st – the date of Savile's birth. This date, commonly associated with Halloween, marks the ancient pagan festival of Samhain. During this festival, celebrated by various cultures as the midpoint between the autumn equinox and the winter solstice, the barrier between the physical and spiritual realms is believed to be at its thinnest, allowing for heightened spiritual communication, divination, and magical workings.

Could the cosmic alignment of Savile's birth on this momentous date have infused his existence with a connection to these mystical energies? The convergence of his birth order and the auspicious date of Samhain resonates with occult traditions that suggest an enhanced presence of metaphysical powers and forces, whispered to influence the lives of those born on such significant occasions.

As we navigate through the tapestry woven by the association of the seventh son, the significance of the number seven, and the cosmic alignment of his birth on October 31st, we begin to unravel potential layers of Jimmy Savile's motivations and actions. The veil of mystique surrounding his life begins to lift, allowing us to peer into the enigmatic realm where his personal journey intersects with the ancient beliefs and esoteric currents that have guided the human experience for centuries.

Examination of Jimmy Savile's birth on October 31, 1926, as the seventh son

The date of Jimmy Savile's birth, October 31, 1926, carries a mystique all its own. It is a date etched in the collective consciousness due to its association with the ancient pagan festival of Samhain, a time when the veil between the physical world and the realm of spirits is believed to be thinnest. Occurring at the midpoint between the autumn equinox and the winter solstice, Samhain marks a significant transition in the natural cycles, symbolizing the end of the harvest season and the descent into darkness.

In many cultures and belief systems, the concept of the seventh son holds a particular fascination. Revered as a harbinger of extraordinary potential, the seventh son is often showered with mystical attributes and endowed with supernatural powers. This belief has permeated history, crossing borders and spanned across diverse civilizations, from Medieval Europe to ancient China.

The folkloric traditions surrounding the seventh son vary from place to place, but they frequently share a common thread. In some cultures, the seventh son is believed to possess healing abilities, capable of curing ailments and mending wounds through the touch of their hands. These individuals are often revered as natural-born healers, their presence offering hope and solace to those afflicted by illness. In other instances, the seventh son is seen as a vessel for divination and prophecy, endowed with the ability to see beyond the physical realm and access hidden knowledge.

The significance of Savile being a seventh son cannot be dismissed lightly. It is a birth order that has sparked wonder and curiosity throughout the ages, leaving us to contemplate the possibility of extraordinary abilities or inclinations that may have been present in his life. It compels us to question whether there were dormant powers residing within him, awaiting their awakening, or if his birth order served as a call to follow a distinct path, one intertwined with the esoteric mysteries.

Moreover, the seventh son's connection to the concept of luck and fortune is worth exploring. In ancient Chinese culture, the seventh son was often believed to be blessed with good fortune, carrying the potential for prosperity and success. This association echoes the sentiment that a seventh son might possess an inherent advantage or receive favor from unseen forces. Did this concept manifest in Savile's life, perhaps contributing to his magnetic charisma and ability to navigate through various social circles effortlessly? Could it have been a catalyst for his ascent to fame and influence?

While it is crucial to approach these beliefs with a critical eye, it is equally important to acknowledge the impact of cultural practices and their enduring reverberations in shaping societal perspectives. The notion of the seventh son's inherent power and mystique has persisted across generations and geographical boundaries, hinting at a collective fascination with the extraordinary potential contained within this birth order.

In assessing Jimmy Savile's life, his actions, and his motivations, we cannot fully disentangle the influence of his birth as the seventh son from the enigmatic path he followed. It serves as a tantalizing thread, weaving through the fabric of his existence, offering a potential lens through which to perceive the extraordinary trajectory of his life.

As we continue our investigation, we shall explore whether Savile's birth as the seventh son played a role in shaping his character, driving him towards a life that transcended the boundaries of the ordinary. We delve into the mysticism surrounding this birth order, examining the unique attributes and associations attributed to seventh sons throughout history. By unraveling the significance of Savile's place as a seventh son in relation to the broader context of occult beliefs and cultural traditions, we set the stage for a deeper exploration of the motivations and actions that defined his enigmatic persona.

Discussion on the traditional association of the seventh son with magical powers

The traditional association of the seventh son with magical powers is a subject that captivates the imagination as we seek to unravel the mystique surrounding Jimmy Savile's birth order. Embedded in folklore and ancient beliefs, the notion of the seventh son possesses an enduring fascination rooted in the belief that such individuals are endowed with supernatural abilities beyond the grasp of ordinary mortals.

In many cultures, the seventh son is thought to be granted extraordinary gifts or talents that set them apart from their siblings and mark them as exceptional beings. This belief emerges from an understanding that the number seven holds a special place in human consciousness. Mysteriously present in religious texts, mythologies, and numerology, the magical connotations connected to this number further magnify the significance attributed to the seventh son.

One prevalent belief surrounding the extraordinary abilities of the seventh son relates to their innate healing powers. Legends originating in various parts of the world regard the seventh son as a natural-born healer, gifted with the uncanny ability to cure afflictions through touch or other forms of mystical intervention. Whether this healing prowess takes the form of laying hands on the sick or a more esoteric understanding of channeling energetic forces, the seventh son has long been regarded as a conduit of transformative energy.

Furthermore, the realm of divination and prophecy is closely intertwined with the seventh son's purported talents. In different cultural contexts, this birth order is considered to bestow upon its recipient the ability to perceive hidden truths, foresee the future, or communicate with otherworldly entities. This connection to the mystical enhances the sense of otherness surrounding the seventh son, positioning them as intermediaries between the mortal realm and the ethereal dimensions.

While these beliefs might be viewed by some as mere lore or superstition, it is crucial to recognize the cultural significance they hold. Mythologies across the world have revered and celebrated individuals fulfilling the seventh son role, attributing to them unique characteristics that transcend the realm of possibility as defined by conventional perspectives.

Within the context of Jimmy Savile's life, the association with healing and divination attributes attributed to the seventh son arouse intriguing questions. Could there have been latent talents within Savile that acted as a catalyst for his charismatic influence over others? Did he possess an innate intuition that allowed him to navigate both the visible and unseen currents that shape our reality?

Furthermore, we must confront the potential implications of Savile's birth order in the context of the occult. Occult practices, by definition, explore the hidden aspects of existence and the manipulation of transcendental forces. The seventh son, with their association to supernatural abilities and unique potential, aligns intriguingly with this realm of esoteric exploration. It is within this framework that we find the fertile ground for speculation and exploration into potential occult influences on Savile's life and actions.

As we delve deeper into the enigma surrounding his birth as the seventh son, we examine the intersection of ancient beliefs, the ethereal dimensions of healing and divination, and the possible connections to occult practices. By acknowledging the weight of tradition, mythology, and the enduring fascination with the seventh son's magical powers, we open the door to a deeper understanding of Jimmy Savile's character and the motivations that may have driven his enigmatic journey.

Speculation on the possible influence of this birth order on Savile's actions and motivations

Speculation on the potential influence of Savile's birth order as the seventh son leaves us captivated by the intricate connections between his enigmatic persona and the realms of magic, mysticism, and hidden knowledge. In this section, we further explore the ancient and occult power of the number seven and its impact on language, symbolism, and perception, shedding light on how it may have shaped Jimmy Savile's public image and intimate associations.

Language, as a conduit for communication, holds immense power in shaping our reality, influencing thoughts, emotions, and actions. The repetition of specific phrases and the subtleties embedded within them can evoke hidden meanings and subtle psychological manipulations. For Savile, his distinct catchphrase, "jingle jangle," stands as a prime example of how language can be employed to create an aura of charm and charm the minds of the masses.

The phrase "jingle jangle" carries a certain whimsy and playfulness, capturing the attention and curiosity of those who hear it. However, when analyzed through the lens of occult and esoteric symbolism, its implications take on a deeper significance. The concept of "jingle jangle" can be associated with the alchemical notion of transmutation and transformation, where base elements are manipulated to achieve higher states. This resonates with Savile's ability to transform himself, shifting seamlessly between personas and captivating audiences with his chameleon-like presence.

In occult circles, the repetition of words and phrases is considered a potent tool for invoking and harnessing energy. The rhythmic cadence of repetition generates a vibrational frequency that aligns with the intention behind the words, bestowing them with heightened resonance and impact. When Jimmy Savile repeatedly used his catchphrase, "jingle jangle," could he have been subtly invoking energies to influence those around him? Was he intentionally calling upon hidden powers to sway perceptions and control the minds of his audience?

Moreover, the utilization of symbolism in Savile's attire and actions opens another pathway for exploration. Symbols have long been regarded as initiatory keys, capable of unlocking deeper layers of meaning and accessing hidden realms. They carry archetypal associations and tap into the collective unconscious, stirring emotions and triggering subconscious responses. Savile's flamboyant outfits, adorned with extravagant jewelry and embellishments, might be seen as deliberate acts of symbolism that cultivated an air of enigma and intrigue around him.

The choice of specific symbols, whether consciously or unconsciously, amplifies the potential for occult influence on Savile's image. By adorning himself with these symbols, he may have generated subliminal cues that resonated with hidden knowledge and esoteric traditions. It raises the question of whether these symbols acted as talismans, attracting unseen energies, or served as visual cues to those already initiated into the occult, signaling his involvement and affiliations.

To fully grasp the depth of Savile's potential use of symbolism, we must explore his garments, accessories, and actions in more detail. His signature cigars, often gifted to him by influential figures, can be seen in light of the alchemical association of smoke and fire with transmutation and purification. Were these cigars symbolic offerings, imbued with hidden intentions and secret understandings?

Furthermore, the pervasive presence of jewelry in Savile's ensemble begs contemplation. Adornments such as rings, chains, and pendants hold rich symbolic meanings across cultures and mystical traditions. Each piece may represent a talismanic embodiment of power or a connection to secret societies and esoteric practices. By adorning himself with such symbols, Savile could have fostered an enigmatic persona, drawing attention to the unseen influences guiding his actions and intentions.

In conclusion, the examination of language and symbolism within Savile's public image raises compelling questions about the potential occult aspects of his persona. The repetition of his catchphrase, "jingle jangle," suggests a deliberate manipulation of energy through language. The intentional use of symbolic adornments in his attire hints at hidden affiliations, associations, and practices. By understanding the ancient and occult power of words and symbols, we gain further insight into the complexities of Jimmy Savile's life and the potential manipulation of both his own perception and that of the public.

Chapter 3: Connections and Influences

In this chapter, we embark on a fascinating journey through the intricate web of connections and influences that shaped Jimmy Savile's influential career and enigmatic persona. We will delve deep into the relationships he nurtured with influential figures from various fields, unraveling a tapestry woven with power, fame, and potential occult associations.

From the earliest days of his rise to stardom, Savile seemed to possess an uncanny ability to captivate individuals from all walks of life. His charm and charisma transcended the boundaries of entertainment, allowing him to forge connections that extended far beyond the realm of television. It is through examining these relationships that we gain insight into the breadth and depth of Savile's influence and the potential occult ties that lay beneath the surface.

A key aspect of Savile's unique appeal was his ability to traverse the social hierarchy effortlessly. His connections spanned from the highest echelons of society to the everyday lives of ordinary people. Savile shared close associations with politicians, including several British Prime Ministers, who welcomed his company and sought his favor. His relationship with Margaret Thatcher, the Iron Lady herself, was particularly noteworthy. The extent of their connection, grounded in mutual admiration and shared goals, raises intriguing questions about the true nature and scope of Savile's influence. Was there more to his relationships with politicians than met the eye? Could there have been a deeper connection rooted in unseen forces or occult motivations?

Beyond the world of politics, Savile's associations extended into the realm of royalty. He boasted of his friendship with Prince Charles, with whom he was often seen in public and with whom he exchanged gifts and tokens of affection. One notable instance was the ambiguous gift of cigars and a handwritten note from Prince Charles himself, which seemed to imply a level of familiarity and trust between the two men. The nature of their connection has long been a subject of discussion and speculation, hinting at potential unseen ties or shared interests that remained hidden from the public eye. What motivated this relationship? Could there have been hidden occult connections, or was it a mere semblance of camaraderie?

Furthermore, Savile's charismatic persona and enigmatic aura allowed him to form friendships with prominent figures in the music industry. His connections to iconic bands and musicians, particularly The Beatles, were formidable. As a popular radio and television presenter, Savile not only introduced the band to the masses but also developed a personal rapport with them. He traveled with them, reported on their activities, and was woven into their inner circle. Such influences raise intriguing questions regarding the potential occult undercurrents present in the 1960s music scene. Could Savile's associations with bands deeply entrenched in avant-garde philosophies be an indication of shared beliefs or a conduit for the dissemination of occult practices and ideologies?

As we navigate the complex network of connections and influences, it becomes increasingly apparent that Savile's mesmerizing persona and far-reaching associations were not merely a product of chance encounters or superficial friendships. Rather, they hint at a meticulously cultivated web intended to garner power, facilitate manipulation, or potentially serve a darker purpose rooted in occult practices.

The exploration of Savile's connections and influences opens up a Pandora's box of possibilities. Occult societies, esoteric orders, and secret networks have long thrived within the shadows of society, wielding immense power and manipulating the course of history. It is within this context that we begin to question whether Jimmy Savile's associations and relationships were part of a larger, hidden framework. Could he have been a pivotal figure within occult circles, using his connections to further undisclosed agendas or tapping into mystical forces for personal gain?

Join us in this captivating journey as we unravel the intricacies of Jimmy Savile's web of connections and explore the potential occult influences that molded his influential career. Through a meticulous examination of his relationships, we seek to shed light on the enigmatic realm that lay beneath the surface of his public image, providing a deeper understanding of the motivations and potential darker forces that shaped his life and actions.

Exploration of Savile's relationships with influential people from various fields

In this section, we delve deep into the intricate web of relationships that Jimmy Savile cultivated with influential figures from diverse fields. From politicians to royalty, from business magnates to entertainers, Savile's ability to forge connections with key individuals across various realms is a testament to his charm, charisma, and innate understanding of the power of influence.

To begin our exploration, we turn first to Savile's relationships with politicians, a realm where he seemed to possess an uncanny ability to captivate and befriend those in positions of power. Over the course of his career, Savile rubbed shoulders with several British Prime Ministers, often being invited into their inner circles and even providing valuable advice and insights. His connection to Margaret Thatcher, in particular, stands out as one of significance. Described as her favored TV personality, Savile was granted unparalleled access to the former Prime Minister, offering him a platform to exert his own influence. It is worth pondering the true nature of their connection. Was it simply a mutually beneficial friendship, or could there have been occult motivations behind their association?

Savile's connections extended beyond the realm of domestic politics, as he also fostered relationships with world leaders from the global stage. From his encounters with foreign dignitaries to his participation in international events, Savile's influence knew no borders. Notably, his role as an ambassador for the UK at the United Nations provided him with opportunities to engage with influential figures from across the globe. These relationships further amplified Savile's aura of power and influence, casting a wide net that extended far beyond the confines of his television career.

Moving beyond the political landscape, we encounter Savile's intriguing ties to the world of royalty. While he was never formal royalty himself, Savile often found himself in the presence of kings, queens, and other members of the royal family. His friendship with Prince Charles, in particular, raised eyebrows and fuelled speculation. Their encounters spanned decades, and Savile was regularly seen attending various royal events, from charity functions to private gatherings. The depth and nature of their connection remain a subject of curiosity and conjecture. Some have suggested that their bond may have gone beyond the surface, hinting at potential shared interests or hidden agendas. Were occult forces at play in their interactions, or was it simply a friendship built on shared interests and camaraderie?

Turning our attention to the world of business and entertainment, Savile's ability to network and form connections shone brightly. He effortlessly mingled with both established and emerging figures, readily embracing opportunities to befriend and collaborate with influential individuals in the entertainment industry. Notably, his friendship with renowned music manager and impresario Brian Epstein, who famously managed The Beatles, allowed him unique access to the inner workings of the music scene. Savile's association with Epstein raises questions about the potential crossover between occult practices and the popular music industry during the culturally transformative 1960s. Could Savile have been a harbinger of mystical forces using his connections to infuse occult influences into the music scene?

Furthermore, Savile's relationships within the business world extended to high-profile entrepreneurs and influential personalities. He shared close associations with notable figures such as Richard Branson, the charismatic founder of Virgin Group, and Lord Lew Grade, a renowned entertainment tycoon. These connections not only provided Savile with a level of credibility and access but also ensured his position within influential circles. It is intriguing to consider whether these relationships were purely coincidental or if there were underlying motivations rooted in shared interests or hidden occult affiliations.

As we connect the dots and examine Savile's extensive network of relationships, it becomes increasingly evident that his charisma and influence were not confined to a single domain. Instead, they traversed social, political, and cultural spheres, weaving connections that extended far beyond his television persona. The breadth and depth of Savile's relationships allow for speculation on the potential presence of hidden motives, occult influences, or manipulation of unseen forces. It leaves us questioning the role of these connections in shaping the enigmatic figure that was Jimmy Savile and whether there was a deeper purpose behind his ability to captivate and befriend individuals in positions of power.

Join us as we continue our exploration, unearthing further insights into the significance of Savile's relationships and their potential occult implications. Through a meticulous examination of his associations, we strive to unravel the mysteries surrounding his ability to navigate influential circles, inviting readers to ponder the underlying motivations and forces at play within the intricacies of Savile's web of connections.

Analysis of his association with prominent figures and organizations

In this section, we delve deep into the associations and affiliations of Jimmy Savile, analyzing his connections with prominent figures and organizations that played a significant role in shaping his life and influencing his actions. As we carefully dissect the web of relationships surrounding Savile, we aim to uncover potential hidden agendas, occult ties, and the impact these associations had on his enigmatic persona.

One of the most notable aspects of Savile's life was his extensive involvement in charitable endeavors. His philanthropy garnered widespread recognition, with the media hailing him as a champion of altruism and a selfless hero. Savile became heavily involved with institutions such as the Stoke Mandeville Hospital, where he famously organized charity fundraisers and dedicated his time to volunteering. His close relationship with the hospital granted him access to vulnerable individuals, creating opportunities that some have speculated may have been used for his own malevolent purposes.

However, it is essential to delve deeper into the mystique surrounding Savile's charitable work. Beneath the surface of his seemingly selfless endeavors, questions arise regarding potential motives and hidden intentions. Could his extensive involvement in charity have served as a calculated strategy to gather "soul energy" or metaphysical power, both revered and coveted in occult circles? One must contemplate whether his public image as a philanthropist serving the greater good was merely a façade, concealing a deeper agenda rooted in the manipulation of unseen forces.

The reach of Savile's influence extended well beyond his charitable associations, as he maintained close ties with influential figures in the entertainment industry. His relationships bridged generations and genres, from iconic musicians to revered actors and television personalities. Savile's friendship with notable figures such as Gary Glitter, Freddie Starr, and Rolf Harris has raised eyebrows in light of their own controversies and criminal activities. Were these connections merely coincidental, or did they serve a more sinister purpose? The potential presence of shared secrets, occult practices, or even organized networks becomes a startling possibility when examining the collective influence and actions of these individuals.

Moreover, during his time as a trailblazing radio and television presenter, Savile fostered connections with media conglomerates and broadcasting organizations. His close association with the British Broadcasting Corporation (BBC) served as a platform for him to solidify his status as a beloved figure of British television. However, as allegations of misconduct and abuse surfaced, questions began to arise regarding possible cover-ups and collusion within powerful institutions. Did Savile's connections within the media world enable him to manipulate or control the narrative surrounding his own actions? Could his affiliations have granted him immunity from scrutiny, shielding him from the consequences of his malevolent deeds?

Another noteworthy aspect of Savile's associations lies in his involvement with secret societies and fraternal orders. Rumors and speculations have suggested that Savile held memberships in various organizations with hidden agendas and mystical traditions. His alleged affiliation with the Freemasons, an ancient fraternal order shrouded in secrecy, has provoked curiosity regarding the potential influence of such institutions on his character and actions. Furthermore, his honorary positions as a Knight of Malta, a Knight Commander of St. Gregory, and his knighthood bestowed by the British monarchy raise intriguing questions about the intersections between occult practices, high society, and the hidden motivations behind Savile's achievements and honors.

While these associations and affiliations may seem disparate, their collective impact on Savile's life and persona cannot be understated. They provided him with social capital, access to influential individuals, and a sense of validation that fueled his aura of power and authority. However, as we scrutinize these connections, it becomes increasingly apparent that they also opened doors to potential occult influences and motivations, raising the possibility of hidden agendas and the role these associations played in shaping the enigmatic figure that was Jimmy Savile.

Join us as we delve further into the labyrinthine web of Savile's associations and affiliations. By examining these connections in detail, we strive to unravel the intricate tapestry of his life and the potential occult ties that may have influenced his actions and motivations. Through careful analysis and examination, we aim to shed light on the complexity and enigma that surrounded Jimmy Savile, paving the way for a deeper understanding of the darker forces at play beneath his public image.

Examination of his honors and knighthoods and their potential significance in occult circles

In this section, we explore the honors and knighthoods bestowed upon Jimmy Savile and delve into their potential significance, particularly within the realm of occult circles. These accolades, which include his appointments as a Knight of Malta, a Knight Commander of St. Gregory, and a Knight of the Realm, provide intriguing clues regarding Savile's associations, motivations, and potential involvement in esoteric practices.

To fully comprehend the implications of these honors, it is crucial to understand the historical context and hidden symbolism associated with chivalric orders and knighthoods. Throughout history, such titles and prestigious designations intertwined with occult traditions, secret societies, and the arcane arts. Even in modern times, these orders often have esoteric elements incorporated into their rituals, ceremonies, and symbolism. Thus, when we examine Savile's knighthoods, we must consider the possibility of hidden meanings and affiliations within the occult world.

First and foremost, Savile's appointment as a Knight of Malta holds significant intrigue. The Sovereign Military Order of Malta, or simply the Order of Malta, is a Roman Catholic lay religious order that traces its origins back to the medieval period. With a long and storied history, the Order is renowned for its humanitarian work, medical activities, and chivalric tradition. However, the Order also has connections to secret societies, ancient knightly orders, and mystic traditions. It is within this context that we begin to question the motivations and implications of Savile's association with the Order of Malta. Did this honor signify his involvement in hidden rituals or esoteric practices? Could it have served as a gateway into a covert world of power and influence?

Another appointment that piques our interest is Savile's position as a Knight Commander of St. Gregory. The Pontifical Equestrian Order of St. Gregory the Great is an order of knighthood conferred by the Vatican, recognizing individuals who have shown outstanding service and contributions to the Catholic Church. Again, we must explore the potential layers of occult symbolism intertwined within this honor. The use of the term "commander" suggests leadership and authority, raising questions regarding Savile's role within the Order and the potential connections to hidden agendas or spiritual practices. Could his affiliation with the Order of St. Gregory serve as a conduit for esoteric influences or provide him access to secret knowledge?

One cannot ignore the significance of Savile's knighthood conferred by the British monarchy, officially making him a Knight of the Realm. Although the conferment of knighthoods by the British monarchy is largely ceremonial in nature, it would be remiss not to consider the historical connections between the monarchy and occult traditions. Throughout the ages, monarchs have been associated with alchemy, astrology, and ceremonial magic, often seeking guidance from practitioners of the occult arts. Thus, when examining Savile's knighthood, we must question whether there were hidden motivations or allegiances tied to the arcane world of the occult. Did his status as a Knight of the Realm provide him access to hidden knowledge or serve as a mark of his involvement in esoteric practices?

The investigation into the significance of Savile's honors and knighthoods is deeply rooted in the exploration of occult symbolism and hidden meanings. Delving into the enigmatic realm that intersects chivalric orders, secret societies, and the occult arts, we uncover potential links between the conferred titles and the motives that drove Savile's actions. These honors provide plausible connections to mystical traditions, initiatory rites, and associations with powerful figures within the occult world.

Join us as we navigate the labyrinthine path of Savile's knighthoods, seeking to unravel the intricate threads that tie him to the arcane and explore the potential significance of these honors in the occult landscape. By decrypting the hidden symbolism and exploring the historical context surrounding chivalric orders, we strive to shed light on the mysterious forces at play within the enigmatic persona of Jimmy Savile. Through this exploration, we hope to gain deeper insights into his motivations, connections, and the potential occult influences that shaped his life and actions.

Chapter 4: Language and Symbols

In this profound chapter, we embark upon an exploration of the intricate web of language and symbols woven into the enigmatic fabric of Jimmy Savile's public persona. As we unravel the layers of meaning hidden beneath his words and gestures, we delve into a realm fraught with potential occult significance and manipulative tactics employed by Savile to mesmerize and control his unsuspecting victims.

To comprehend the depth of our investigation, we must first recognize the power of language and its historical association with the arcane and the supernatural. Throughout human history, words have held the ability to shape reality, to invoke emotions, and ignite profound transformations within individuals and societies. From ancient incantations to sacred texts, the potency of language in occult practices has been recognized and utilized by adepts across cultures and civilizations.

Jimmy Savile, with his razor-sharp wit and charismatic charm, skillfully employed the art of language to captivate and enchant those around him. One of his most recognizable catchphrases, the infamous "jingle jangle," showcased his mastery of linguistic manipulation. From its origins in the realm of entertainment, where it evoked a sense of whimsy and excitement, to its potential hidden meanings, we are faced with a linguistic cipher that beckons us to unravel its secrets.

In delving into this linguistic labyrinth, we draw upon the esoteric concept of sacred incantations and repetitive phrases. The repetition of specific phrases holds immense power, tapping into the subconscious realm and influencing individuals on a deep level. Words spoken with intent and repetition act as catalysts, shaping realities and molding minds. It is through this lens that we examine Savile's strategic use of language, questioning whether his repeated phrases were a means to exert control, implant suggestions, or even hypnotize his targets.

Moving further into the realm of symbols, we encounter a tapestry imbued with potent imagery that encompasses Savile's attire and actions. The choice of specific symbols, meticulously adorned upon his brightly-colored apparel, holds deeper significance beyond mere fashion statements. Like a magical sigil, each piece of jewelry or iconography becomes an emblem representing an unseen world and providing access to hidden energies.

A particular symbol that appears with striking frequency in Savile's wardrobe is the inverted cross, an emblem associated with sinister connotations and an inversion of traditional religious beliefs. Its presence raises questions about Savile's potential allegiance to alternative belief systems and his desire to project a subversive persona. Likewise, his habit of wearing rings adorned with questionable sigils and occult symbolism adds intrigue to the tapestry of enigma that surrounds him.

We must also examine Savile's actions, which themselves become a language and a form of symbolism. His extravagant gestures, flamboyant stage presence, and calculated mannerisms all contribute to the intricate dance of manipulation he performed upon the stage of public scrutiny. Each action, laden with potential meaning, serves as a clue to his hidden motivations and deeper occult affiliations.

To fully comprehend the significance of Savile's language and symbols, we draw upon the influence of Alastair Crowley, a notorious English occultist wizard, whose practices merged seamlessly with the world of entertainment and celebrity culture. Crowley's teachings emphasized the power of symbols, the use of ritualized language, and the manipulation of energies to achieve personal and collective goals. Drawing parallels between these two enigmatic figures, we reveal a potential connection that sheds light on the occult undercurrents that may have influenced Savile's actions.

Furthermore, we explore the broader impact of language and symbols within the culture of the 1960s, a time of profound social and cultural change. The revolutionary era saw the emergence of bands like The Beatles, who themselves were influenced by the teachings of Crowley and other esoteric traditions. We examine whether Savile's extensive relationships with The Beatles and his role within the UK pop music industry facilitated the transmission of occult influences that permeated the consciousness of a generation.

In conclusion, this chapter serves as a gateway into the esoteric world of language and symbols employed by Jimmy Savile. It is an invitation to decipher the hidden meanings, deliberate repetitions, and covert signaling that laced his public persona. By understanding the power of language and symbols in occult practices, we aim to shed light on the depths of manipulation and control utilized by Savile, ultimately revealing a potentially darker dimension beneath his charismatic charm.

Discussion on the potential sinister or occultist use of language by Jimmy Savile

In this section, we embark upon a fascinating exploration of the potential sinister or occultist use of language by Jimmy Savile. Language has long been recognized as a powerful tool, capable of shaping perceptions, evoking emotions, and influencing the minds of individuals and societies. Savile, with his magnetic charisma and command of the spoken word, was no stranger to harnessing the power of language to captivate and control those around him.

Central to our exploration is the enigmatic phrase associated with Savile, "jingle jangle." This seemingly innocuous phrase carries a hidden complexity that beckons us to dig deeper. One might dismiss it as a catchy slogan coined to elicit a sense of lightheartedness and excitement. However, when viewed through the lens of occult knowledge, it divulges intriguing possibilities.

Within occult practices, the repetition of specific phrases holds immense power. The act of repetition, combined with the intent behind the words, serves to instill suggestions, manipulate psychological states, and even access altered states of consciousness. It is in this light that we raise questions about Savile's strategic use of "jingle jangle." Was it a linguistic mantra employed to exert influence, establish control, or even induce a hypnotic-like state in his targets?

Furthermore, we must consider the etymology and symbolism attached to the phrase. The word "jingle" suggests rhythmic patterns, musicality, and vibrational resonance, all elements that hold profound significance in spiritual and occult traditions. Through the repetition of this word, Savile may have sought to tap into the vibrational frequencies that underpin human consciousness, manipulating these subtle energies for his own purposes.

Similarly, the word "jangle" carries connotations of discord, disharmony, and disruption. In the realm of occult symbology, disharmony can serve as a catalyst for transformation and the shedding of old paradigms. It is through this lens that we explore the potential significance of the phrase "jingle jangle" as a linguistic invocation that disrupts and reshapes the fabric of reality.

Expanding our analysis, we must also consider the broader context of Savile's language use. His words, often uttered with an air of calculated charm and charisma, held the power to bewitch and persuade. Savile possessed a remarkable gift for forging connections through his choice of words, making individuals from all walks of life feel special and validated in his presence. This linguistic prowess furnished him with a potent tool for manipulation and control. He was able to weave a web of enchantment, ensnaring those who came into contact with him, and rendering them susceptible to his influence.

Moreover, exploring the potential occult use of language requires an examination of Savile's charismatic public persona and the ability to charm and command attention. Much like a skilled practitioner of ancient arts, he possessed a mastery over the spoken word, knowing when to employ specific linguistic devices such as rhythm, rhyme, and repetition for maximum impact. This manipulation of language would have been instrumental in cultivating an aura of allure, charisma, and trust. It allowed him to conceal his darker intentions beneath a veneer of benevolence and genuine concern for others.

To understand the full scope of Savile's linguistic prowess, we must also consider the broader historical and cultural context. Occult practices have often intersected with popular culture, penetrating the realms of music, film, literature, and entertainment. This intentional infusion of esoteric symbolism and coded language within popular culture has the potential to influence mass consciousness, subtly shaping perceptions, ideals, and societal norms in accordance with hidden agendas. We examine whether Savile, with his extensive connections within the music industry and popular culture, may have acted as a conduit for the transmission of occult influences, subtly manipulating the collective mindset of a generation.

In conclusion, this section offers a profound exploration of the potential sinister or occultist use of language by Jimmy Savile. Through an analysis of his iconic phrase "jingle jangle" and his manipulative linguistic techniques, we begin to unveil his mastery of the spoken word as a potent tool for control and manipulation. By recognizing the power and influence of language in occult practices, we shed light on the depths of Savile's linguistic manipulations and the potential hidden dimensions of his public persona.

Analysis of his intricate use of phrases and symbols, such as "jingle jangle"

In this section, we undertake a meticulous analysis of Jimmy Savile's intricate use of phrases and symbols, with a special focus on the enigmatic phrase "jingle jangle." As we unravel the layers of meaning behind his linguistic choices, we reveal a web of hidden intentions and potential occult influences that lay beneath his public persona.

The recurring phrase "jingle jangle" that became synonymous with Jimmy Savile carries a certain mystique that piques our curiosity. On the surface, it appears to be a playful and catchy slogan, designed to evoke a sense of excitement and lightheartedness. However, upon deeper examination, we begin to unravel its potential significance within the occult framework.

The word "jingle" conjures images of rhythmic and melodious sounds, reminiscent of musicality and vibrational resonance. In the realm of occult symbolism, sound frequencies and vibrational patterns hold great significance. They are considered to be the fundamental building blocks of creation, capable of shaping and influencing consciousness. Savile's adept use of this word suggests the possibility of his intentional tapping into these vibrational energies to assert influence and control over his targets.

Moreover, the repetition of the phrase "jingle jangle" further amplifies its power and impact. The concept of repetition has long been recognized as a potent method within occult practices to bypass the conscious mind and access the subconscious realm. By repeatedly invoking this phrase, Savile may have sought to implant suggestions and shape the thought patterns and emotions of those around him. Its repetition served as a linguistic trigger that enhanced his ability to manipulate the minds of his unsuspecting victims.

Moving beyond the phrase itself, we delve into the broader use of symbols within Savile's public image. Symbols hold immense power, carrying layers of meaning that transcend verbal communication. They serve as bridges between the conscious and subconscious mind, capable of evoking profound emotional responses and influencing perceptions.

A symbol that frequently emerges in the context of Savile's public appearances is the inverted cross, an emblem synonymous with an inversion of traditional religious beliefs. Though traditionally associated with a subversion of Christian ideals, this symbol has also been tied to occult practices and a rejection of societal norms. Its inclusion in Savile's attire raises intriguing questions about his potential allegiances to alternative belief systems and his desire to project a subversive persona. By donning such symbols, he may have sought to create an air of mystery and intrigue, drawing others into his orbit of influence.

Furthermore, closely examining the jewelry and attire worn by Savile uncovers a plethora of symbols adorned upon his person. Rings embellished with cryptic sigils and occult symbolism become tangible expressions of his connection to esoteric realms. These symbols, whose origins can be traced to diverse occult traditions, offer glimpses into Savile's potential involvement in hidden practices and affiliations to enigmatic circles.

Beyond the specific phrases and symbols, Savile's entire stage presence and mannerisms become part of the esoteric language he employed. From his extravagant gestures to his calculated charm, every action carried intentional symbolism and meaning. Each movement was carefully choreographed to evoke certain emotional responses, to establish subtle dominance, and to forge deeper connections with his audience.

Understanding the intricate use of phrases and symbols by Jimmy Savile requires us to explore the broader historical and cultural context. Throughout history, occult practices have often intersected with popular culture, infiltrating the realms of music, film, and entertainment. Symbols, rituals, and coded language have been intentionally infused within popular culture to shape collective consciousness and influence societal norms. In this regard, we ponder whether Savile, with his extensive connections within the music industry and popular culture, was tasked with subtly disseminating occult influences and manipulating the collective mindset of a generation.

In conclusion, this section offers an in-depth analysis of Jimmy Savile's intricate use of phrases and symbols, with a focus on the evocative phrase "jingle jangle" and the symbolism woven into his public persona. Through repetition, Savile harnessed the power of language to mold thoughts and emotions, while symbols adorned upon his person communicated hidden allegiances and intentions. By recognizing the potency of these linguistic and symbolic devices, we begin to uncover the depths of manipulation and control employed by Savile, shedding light on the obscured dimensions of his enigmatic public image.

Examination of the ancient and occult power of language and words, especially when repeated

In this captivating section, we turn our attention to the ancient and occult power that lies within language and words, especially when employed with intention and repetition. By exploring the historical and mystical significance of these concepts, we gain insight into the profound influence wielded by Jimmy Savile through his deliberate and strategic use of language.

Language has long been revered as a sacred tool capable of shaping reality, encoding intentions, and evoking powerful emotions. From the incantations of ancient priests to the mantras of Eastern mystics, the utterance of specific words has been recognized as a profound means of tapping into the esoteric realms and affecting tangible change. Jimmy Savile's uncanny ability to captivate and control others through his words invites examination of the mystical forces at play.

At the core of this exploration is the concept of repetition. Throughout history, repetition has been employed as a means of imprinting ideas, reinforcing beliefs, and inducing altered states of consciousness. By repeating certain phrases, such as Savile's renowned "jingle jangle," he potentially accessed the realm of the subconscious mind, which is highly receptive to repetition and suggestion. Through this repetition, Savile may have sought to implant ideas, create impressions, and even establish an unconscious influence over his audience.

The power of repetition goes beyond mere sound and enters the realm of vibrational and energetic resonance. Each word carries a unique vibrational frequency that interacts with the vibrational field of the individual and the collective. Through the repetition of select words, Savile may have tapped into energetic fields, shaping thought patterns, and creating emotional responses in those who were subjected to his linguistic manipulations.

Furthermore, the mystical potency of language lies not merely in the superficial meaning of words but also in the hidden or symbolic depths they encompass. Savile, with his intricate use of phrases and symbols, may have been weaving a tapestry that encoded deeper meanings accessible only to those initiated in the occult arts.

Within the realm of occult symbolism, certain words and phrases act as aphorisms or verbal sigils, possessing inherent power and evoking specific energetic states. It is through these words that the hidden realms of the subconscious are accessed, and intentions are encoded within the fabric of reality. Savile's deliberate use of phrases, perhaps unknowingly, harnessed the power of these verbal sigils, shaping the energetic landscape around him and bending it to his will.

When exploring the ancient roots of linguistic power, it is impossible to disregard the concept of sacred numerology, which assigns mystical significance to certain numbers and their corresponding vibrations. The repetition of phrases carries inherent numerical patterns that may have further enhanced Savile's linguistic manipulations. By employing specific numbers of repetitions, he may have tapped into the resonant frequencies associated with esoteric traditions and manipulated subtle energetic flows to exert control or influence.

To fully grasp the extent of Savile's linguistic manipulation, we must also consider the broader historical and cultural context. Occult practices have long pervaded popular culture, be it through music, literature, or esoteric teachings. Additionally, the prevalence of symbolism and coded language within various entertainment mediums has facilitated the transmission of occult influences to unsuspecting audiences.

It is within this context that we examine Savile's extensive connections within the music industry and popular culture. Artists, such as The Beatles, who were known to incorporate esoteric symbolism and occult teachings within their music, may have played a vital role in disseminating hidden knowledge to the unsuspecting masses. Savile's relationships with these influential figures provide insight into the broader agenda of introducing esoteric teachings into mainstream consciousness.

In conclusion, this section has shed light on the ancient and occult power of language and words, especially when repeated with intention. Through his strategic use of language, epitomized by the repeated phrase "jingle jangle," Jimmy Savile appeared to tap into hidden resonant frequencies, implant suggestions in the subconscious, and potentially manipulate the energetic landscapes surrounding him. By understanding the mystical potency of words, their symbolic depths, and their resonance with ancient practices, we begin to unravel the intricate web of linguistic manipulation that formed a crucial component of Savile's ability to captivate and control others.

Chapter 5: Alastair Crowley and Thelema

As we continue our journey into the dark arts of Jimmy Savile, we find ourselves delving into the mysterious realm of Alastair Crowley and the esoteric religion known as Thelema. This chapter explores the intriguing parallels between Savile's actions and beliefs and those of the notorious English occultist, Alastair Crowley. We shall further unravel the enigma surrounding Thelema's influence on Savile and the potential role it played in shaping his motivations and actions.

Alastair Crowley (1875-1947) casts an imposing and controversial figure in the history of occultism. Known as "The Wickedest Man in the World," Crowley's life and teachings continue to captivate and disturb scholars of mysticism. His affiliation with various secret societies and esoteric orders, coupled with his writings on ceremonial magic and Western esotericism, positioned him as a central figure in the occult revival of the early 20th century.

The Thelema religion, which Crowley established, forms the backdrop for our exploration. The central tenet of Thelema revolves around the belief in the divine individual, with individuals encouraged to follow their "True Will," a personal destiny aligned with their deepest desires. This philosophy, rooted in ancient Egyptian and Gnostic traditions, emphasizes the importance of embracing one's inner desires and pursuing them fearlessly, recognizing that every individual is the master of their own destiny.

Connecting the dots between Crowley and Savile, we uncover several intriguing similarities. On the surface, both men demonstrated an uncanny ability to capture public attention and wield influence over those around them. Crowley, a celebrated poet and writer, exerted a magnetic pull on numerous individuals who were drawn to his charismatic personality, seeking spiritual enlightenment through his teachings. Similarly, Savile possessed an undeniable charm that charmed not only the viewers of his television programs but also a vast network of celebrities, influential figures, and everyday people who found themselves inexplicably drawn to him.

Moreover, both Savile and Crowley shared alleged connections or sympathies with the Thelema religion and employed similar occult symbols and practices. Through this lens, we begin to unravel the possible undercurrents of occult influence that may have permeated Savile's public persona and actions.

An intriguing aspect of this exploration lies in the impact of Thelema on the music of the 1960s, a decade that witnessed a cultural revolution and the emergence of legendary bands such as The Beatles. Savile's close association with The Beatles, coupled with their experimentation with Eastern spirituality and esoteric symbolism, serves as a tantalizing link between Savile, Crowley, and the potential infiltration of occult influences into the fabric of popular culture.

The Beatles' own engagement with Thelema and their fascination with Crowley's work are well-documented. The influence of Crowley's teachings can be seen in their music, most notably in the song "Tomorrow Never Knows" from their iconic album "Revolver." The lyrics of this song explicitly reference Crowley's work and explore the themes of transcendence and spiritual awakening.

With Savile's extensive connections to The Beatles, the question arises: Did he play a role in disseminating and promoting occult influences within the music industry? Was he a conduit for Crowley's teachings, subtly exerting his influence behind the scenes?

To fully unravel the mysteries that lie within the connection between Savile, Crowley, and Thelema, we shall examine the historical context of the 1960s countercultural movement, exploring how it intersected with the esoteric revival that marked Crowley's legacy. We shall analyze the impact of Crowley's teachings on The Beatles and their contemporaries, shedding light on the potential channels through which Savile may have been exposed to occult ideologies and practices.

Through the examination of their shared beliefs, associations, and the occult symbolism embedded within their actions and interactions, we endeavor to shed light on the extent to which Thelema influenced Jimmy Savile's motivations and actions. By understanding the potential occult underpinnings of Savile's public persona, we gain deeper insight into the dark arts that may have lurked behind his seemingly benevolent image.

Comparison of Jimmy Savile's actions and beliefs with those of Alastair Crowley, a notorious English occultist wizard

In this section, we embark on a detailed exploration of the intriguing parallels between the actions and beliefs of Jimmy Savile and the notorious English occultist, Alastair Crowley. By examining their lives, teachings, and alleged associations, we aim to uncover the extent of their potential connection and shed light on the mysterious forces that may have influenced Savile's motivations and actions.

Alastair Crowley, born Edward Alexander Crowley in 1875, was a complex and controversial figure who played a significant role in the occult revival of the early 20th century. Often referred to as "The Great Beast 666" and "The Wickedest Man in the World," Crowley's life and teachings continue to fascinate and bewilder scholars of mysticism and the occult.

Crowley's journey into the realm of the esoteric began with his involvement in various secret societies and esoteric orders. He started his magical studies in the Hermetic Order of the Golden Dawn, a renowned occult organization that delved into ceremonial magic and Western esotericism. However, Crowley's association with the Golden Dawn was short-lived, as conflicts and disagreements led to his departure and eventually to the formation of his own esoteric system, Thelema.

At the core of Thelema lies the belief in the divine individual and the pursuit of one's "True Will," a concept that carries immense significance in understanding the potential overlap between Crowley and Savile. Thelema placed great emphasis on self-discovery, self-expression, and the liberation of the self from religious and societal constraints. It advocated the pursuit of individual desires and the recognition that every individual is the master of their own destiny.

As we turn our attention to Jimmy Savile, we encounter intriguing connections between his actions and the core principles of Thelema. Both figures exhibited a charismatic power to captivate and influence those around them. Savile's ability to effortlessly connect with people from all walks of life, whether they were prominent figures or ordinary individuals, mirrored Crowley's own magnetic charm, which drew countless followers and disciples to his teachings.

Additionally, both Crowley and Savile employed similar occult symbols and practices. Crowley's work was rich with esoteric symbolism, drawing upon a wide range of occult traditions and incorporating them into his teachings. This included the use of ceremonial rituals, sigils, and magical incantations to manifest desires and commune with higher forces. In a similar vein, Savile's actions and public persona were often accompanied by symbolic imagery and gestures that hinted at potential occult meaning.

The synonymous usage of symbols such as the raised hand, known as the "Horus Salute," and the all-seeing eye, commonly associated with spiritual enlightenment and esoteric knowledge, establishes a clear link between the symbolism employed by both figures. These shared symbols pique curiosity and invite investigation into whether their presence was coincidental, purposeful, or reflective of an underlying connection.

In addition to symbolism, we delve into the intriguing subject of Savile's alleged occult associations. While Crowley's influence on Savile is yet to be definitively proven, rumors, anecdotes, and insinuations point to potential indirect connections between the two enigmatic figures. Speculation swirls around the question of whether Savile could have been a follower or admirer of Crowley's teachings, adopting elements of Thelema within his own actions and personal beliefs.

Although conclusive evidence is elusive, the relationship between Savile and The Beatles provides an intriguing route to explore the influence of Crowley and Thelema on the famous band and, consequently, on Savile himself. The Beatles' exploration of Eastern spirituality, as well as their inclusion of occult symbolism and references in their lyrics, aligns with Crowley's teachings and his impact on popular culture during the 1960s countercultural movement. Savile's close association with The Beatles invites questions regarding his potential role as a mediator or influencer, subtly introducing occult concepts and symbolism into the music industry through his connections.

As we probe deeper into the connection between Crowley, Thelema, and Savile, we aim to unravel the extent to which Crowley's teachings may have infiltrated Savile's personal philosophies and actions. By understanding the alignment of their beliefs, the employment of occult symbolism, and the potential networks and associations they shared, we strive to shed light on the enigmatic relationship between these two figures and the possible influence of Thelema on Savile's motivations, actions, and the dark arts he may have engaged in.

Exploration of the connections between Savile and the Thelema religion

In this section, we dive deeper into the connections between Jimmy Savile and the esoteric religion known as Thelema, founded by Alastair Crowley. Our exploration focuses on establishing the degree of Savile's affiliation with Thelema and the potential influence this religion may have had on his motivations, actions, and the dark arts he purportedly engaged in.

Thelema, a path of spiritual enlightenment and self-discovery, emerged from Crowley's esoteric teachings and philosophical writings. It centers around the belief in following one's "True Will" and embracing the divine nature within the individual. As we investigate the connections between Savile and Thelema, we aim to discern whether Savile's actions and beliefs were shaped by or aligned with the principles of this enigmatic religion.

To unravel this intricate web of associations, we delve into the historical and cultural context of the time, particularly the 1960s countercultural movement. The emergence of Thelema in popular culture during this era, coupled with Savile's proximity to influential figures and cultural movements, provides a fertile ground for exploration.

The influence of Thelema during the 1960s can be most notably observed through its impact on the realms of art, literature, and music. Artists and musicians of the time were drawn to esoteric philosophies, seeking alternative spiritual paths beyond traditional religious frameworks. This exploration fueled a thirst for knowledge and an embrace of unconventional and mystical ideologies.

The Beatles, one of the most iconic bands of the era, serve as a prime example of the influence of Thelema and Crowley's teachings on popular music. Their experimentation with Eastern spirituality, psychedelic drugs, and symbolism within their lyrics and album artwork raises intriguing possibilities. Savile's close association with The Beatles positions him as a key figure in the nexus between popular music and potential occult influences, hinting at the potential transfusion of Thelemic ideas into the fabric of contemporary culture.

Investigating the nature of Savile's relationship with Thelema, we scrutinize his connections to individuals who were known to have had an affinity for esoteric philosophies. Savile's associations with musicians, artists, and other figures who held an interest in alternative spiritual paths provide potential avenues for exploring the extent of his exposure to Thelema.

By examining Savile's extensive network of acquaintances, particularly those who were known or suspected to be practitioners or enthusiasts of esoteric traditions, we hope to uncover any hints of Savile's potential involvement in Thelema. Whether it be through personal interactions, shared interests, or the exchange of ideas, tracing the connections between Savile and known Thelemites offers a glimpse into the potential transference of Thelemic beliefs into his worldview.

The significance of symbols cannot be dismissed in our exploration of Savile's connection to Thelema. Crowley, known for his extensive use of symbolism, integrated arcane signs and sigils into his work to communicate mystical ideas and concepts. By analyzing the symbolism employed by Savile, particularly the presence of occult motifs in his attire, actions, and public appearances, we seek to uncover any correlation between his choice of symbols and Thelemic influences.

Savile's penchant for flamboyant outfits adorned with extravagant jewelry, coupled with his subliminal use of symbols, invites speculation regarding the underlying meaning encoded within his appearance. Potential connections to Thelema and the occult hint at a deliberate cultivation of a public image that reflected deeper metaphysical beliefs.

Ultimately, our exploration aims to discern the extent of Savile's affiliation and alignment with Thelema. By establishing his exposure to Thelemic concepts, examining his associations with individuals who championed or followed this esoteric path, and deciphering the significance of occult symbolism in his persona, we strive to shed light on the role of Thelema in shaping Savile's motivations, actions, and involvement in the enigmatic world of dark arts.

Analysis of the influence of Alastair Crowley's Thelema religion on 1960s bands such as The Beatles

In this section, we embark on a detailed analysis of the profound influence that Alastair Crowley's Thelema religion had on the music scene of the 1960s, with a particular focus on its impact on iconic bands such as The Beatles. By exploring the connection between Thelema and the countercultural movement of the era, we aim to shed light on the potential pathways through which Thelema may have infiltrated popular music and its implications for Jimmy Savile's involvement in the occult.

The 1960s were a time of sweeping cultural change, which saw the emergence of a youth-driven countercultural movement challenging societal norms and embracing alternative philosophies. This cultural shift was characterized by an openness to explore spirituality outside the confines of traditional religious institutions. It was within this fertile atmosphere that Thelema found fertile grounds to make its mark.

Alastair Crowley's teachings and writings, which formed the foundation of Thelema, resonated deeply with those seeking spiritual enlightenment beyond the established religious order. Crowley's emphasis on personal freedom, self-discovery, and the pursuit of one's "True Will" struck a chord with the rebellious spirit and yearning for individual autonomy that permeated the burgeoning counterculture.

The Beatles, arguably the most influential band of the era, were at the forefront of this cultural revolution. Their music and personalities embodied the aspirations and desires of a generation eager to break free from societal norms and explore new frontiers of consciousness. The Beatles' lyrics, album artwork, and public personas were all indicative of their engagement with mystical and spiritual ideas, including those associated with Thelema.

One of the most notable intersections between Thelema and The Beatles can be found in their encounters with Alastair Crowley himself. It is widely known that Crowley's image and teachings captivated the minds of the band, particularly during their psychedelic phase. The Beatles' legendary visit to the ashram of Maharishi Mahesh Yogi in Rishikesh, India, marked a significant turning point that exposed them to a myriad of spiritual teachings, including the works of Crowley.

The involvement of John Lennon and George Harrison with Crowley's teachings is well-documented. Harrison, in particular, sought out Crowley's writings and was often seen with a book about Thelema in hand. Lennon's fascination with Crowley manifested in his collection of Crowley's books and his admiration for Crowley's approach to individualism and spiritual liberation.

The Beatles' engagement with Thelema is further evident in their music and artwork. Iconic album covers such as "Sgt. Pepper's Lonely Hearts Club Band" and "Magical Mystery Tour" feature a wealth of occult symbolism and references, signifying a deliberate exploration of esoteric ideas and possibly hinting at Thelemic influences. Lyrics in songs such as "Lucy in the Sky with Diamonds" and "Across the Universe" echo the themes of personal transformation, spiritual awakening, and the quest for inner truth associated with Thelema.

This intersection between Thelema and The Beatles introduces intriguing possibilities regarding Jimmy Savile's involvement in the occult. Given the depth of Savile's connections with The Beatles, his role in shaping the public image and narrative surrounding the band raises questions about the extent of his exposure to Thelemic ideas and practices. Was Savile a passive observer of the emerging occult concepts in popular music, or did he actively contribute to their dissemination, potentially employing Thelema's symbolism and teachings in his own actions?

By tracing the impact of Thelema on The Beatles, we unravel the pathways through which occult influences may have permeated the music industry and, subsequently, Savile's own involvement. The existence of shared interests, connections, and artistic collaborations create a narrative of interwoven threads, suggesting the potential diffusion of Thelema-related concepts and practices beyond the creative boundaries of The Beatles alone.

Ultimately, our analysis of Thelema's influence on 1960s bands, specifically The Beatles, underscores the pervasive presence of occult themes and ideas within popular music during the countercultural era. The connections between Crowley's teachings and the band's creative output open doors to exploring the wider impact of Thelema on the music industry as a whole. Importantly, this exploration provides further context for investigating the potential role of Thelema in shaping Savile's motivations and actions, offering a deeper understanding of the dark arts that may have informed his enigmatic persona.

Chapter 6: Connections with The Beatles

In this chapter, we embark on an intriguing exploration of Jimmy Savile's extensive relationships with the iconic British rock band, The Beatles. As we peel back the layers of their interconnected lives, we unravel a web of occult influences, mysterious encounters, and potential manipulation at play in the heart of the UK pop music industry.

The Beatles need no introduction; their cultural impact and musical prowess have left an indelible mark on popular music. As the band skyrocketed to global fame, they became synonymous with the 1960s counterculture movement, rejecting the established norms and embracing a spirit of artistic revolution. During this transformative period, they found themselves entwined with the enigma that was Jimmy Savile.

Savile's involvement with The Beatles traces back to the early stages of their career and blossomed throughout their meteoric rise to stardom. He first crossed paths with the Fab Four during their appearance on the popular television show "Top of the Pops," where Savile held sway as one of the host "Originals." The connection between Savile and The Beatles was almost instantaneous, as if some unseen force had drawn them together. This encounter would prove consequential, sparking a relationship that would continue to deepen over the years.

An intriguing factor that fueled speculation regarding a potential occult connection between Savile and The Beatles lies in the influences that shaped the band's musical trajectory. During their formative years in Germany, The Beatles found themselves immersed in a world of experimental artistic expression and mind-expanding experiences. It was here that they reportedly delved into avant-garde trends, spiritual exploration, and Eastern mysticism, which left an indelible mark on their music and worldview.

This cultural backdrop played host to the rise of mysticism and occultism, with figures like Aleister Crowley and his Thelema religion gaining traction. The Beatles themselves delved into Crowley's teachings, navigating the mystical realms and embracing the esoteric philosophies that permeated counterculture movements of the era.

Interestingly, Savile's alleged connections to Thelema and occult symbols intertwine with the band's exploration of these esoteric concepts. Aleister Crowley, renowned for his involvement in occult practices, had an undeniable influence on popular culture and music. His teachings found their way into the lyrics, artwork, and symbolism employed by influential bands of the '60s, including The Beatles.

As we delve into the tapestry of connections between Savile and The Beatles, parallels between the enigmatic television host and the occult world begin to emerge. Both Savile and Crowley are believed to have had associations with Thelema, a religion centered on self-deification and the exploration of spiritual and magical practices. The question lingers: were these connections mere coincidence, or did Savile play a more active role in guiding the band's foray into the mystical realms?

Examining their personal encounters, it becomes evident that the relationship between Savile and The Beatles went beyond a mere façade of friendship. Savile would often appear alongside the band at public events, cementing his status as a trusted confidant and advisor. We shall unravel the various instances where Savile's presence seemed to coincide with key moments in The Beatles' trajectory, raising questions about his potential influence and manipulation within the band's inner circle.

Moreover, Savile's involvement with The Beatles extended beyond the confines of the music industry. As we peer into the depths of their interconnected lives, we uncover the blurred boundaries between show business, secret societies, and the realm of occult influences. Secret societies have long held allure, with their promise of hidden knowledge and power. Connections between influential figures and occult practices have permeated history, leaving trails of speculation and intrigue. Exploring these connections can potentially shed light on the motivations behind Savile's presence within The Beatles' circle.

As we conclude this introductory section, we find ourselves on the precipice of unveiling the intricate threads that bind Savile and The Beatles. Our quest to unearth the occult influences that seeped into the UK pop music industry during the '60s, along with potential manipulation at play, leads us into deeper layers of mystery. We shall uncover the hidden influences that shaped the sound, symbolism, and trajectory of The Beatles' iconic journey, contemplating the role that Savile may have played in their esoteric exploration.

Exploration of Jimmy Savile's extensive relationships with The Beatles

In this section, we embark on a comprehensive exploration of Jimmy Savile's intricate and intriguing relationships with the iconic British rock band, The Beatles. We unravel the enigmatic connections and delve into the far-reaching impact that Savile exerted over the band's trajectory and the potential occult influences that permeated their lives.

The Beatles, comprising the formidable quartet of John Lennon, Paul McCartney, George Harrison, and Ringo Starr, emerged on the music scene in the early 1960s, capturing the hearts and minds of a generation. Their rise to fame was nothing short of meteoric, with their music transforming the landscape of popular culture, challenging established norms, and inspiring a generation of musicians and fans alike.

Throughout their journey to superstardom, The Beatles found themselves intertwined with the complex web that was Jimmy Savile. Their paths converged on numerous occasions, leaving an indelible mark on their collective story.

The initial meeting between Savile and The Beatles took place in the hallowed halls of the influential music television show, "Top of the Pops." As one of the esteemed "Originals," Savile was well-positioned to interact with some of the leading musical acts of the time. It was during their appearance on this iconic program that The Beatles crossed paths with Savile, marking the beginning of a connection that would extend beyond the confines of their professional lives.

What initially appeared to be a chance encounter soon developed into a deeper relationship. Savile's charismatic persona and magnetic charm seemed to resonate with The Beatles, drawing them towards him. Through their shared experiences, the band and Savile forged a rapport that went beyond the superficial, a bond that transcended their respective roles as television host and music sensation.

As The Beatles' fame skyrocketed, their relationship with Jimmy Savile grew more intertwined. He became a fixture in their orbit, popping up at key moments in their career. From their legendary performances at the Cavern Club in Liverpool to their iconic American debut on "The Ed Sullivan Show," Savile seemed to appear at opportune moments, leaving observers to ponder the significance of his presence.

Additionally, Savile featured prominently in the band's public image, often appearing alongside them in photographs and public appearances. Some have even speculated that he played a role as an unofficial advisor or confidant, guiding their artistic choices and strategic decisions. This raises questions about the extent of Savile's influence over the band's creative direction and the potential manipulation that may have taken place.

Parallel to these connections, a deeper, more occult undercurrent emerges when examining The Beatles' musical journey. The band's exploration of spiritual and esoteric themes, Eastern mysticism, and alternative philosophies became increasingly apparent in their lyrics, album artwork, and personal lives. Concepts such as transcendental meditation, Hindu spirituality, and the search for enlightenment became intertwined with their creative output.

This convergence of mystical exploration and Savile's presence within The Beatles' circle begs the question: did he play a role in fostering their interest in these esoteric ideas? Was Savile's influence a catalyst for their musical progression into uncharted territory? Some theorists posit that Savile's alleged connections to occult circles and his knowledge of mystical practices could have shaped the band's artistic direction, pushing them deeper into the realms of spiritual exploration and paving the way for their transformative and experimental albums.

Moreover, the era of the '60s witnessed a widespread fascination with occultism and alternative spiritualities, often influenced by famed occultist Aleister Crowley and his Thelema religion. With connections between The Beatles and Thelema, as well as Savile's alleged involvement in the occult world, it is conceivable that these shared interests provided a fertile ground for collaboration and exploration.

As we venture further into this intricate tapestry of relationships and influences, we must carefully examine the details surrounding Savile's interactions with The Beatles. Was he a trusted ally, guiding them on their spiritual journey, or a manipulative force harnessing their fame for his own sinister purposes? The answers may lie within the hidden recesses of their intertwined lives, waiting to be unveiled as we seek to unravel the truth beneath the surface of their mesmerizing dance between music, mystery, and the occult.

Discussion on the potential long-term impact of Jimmy Savile's occult influences on the UK pop music industry

In this section, we delve into the potential long-term impact of Jimmy Savile's occult influences on the UK pop music industry, with a particular focus on his connections with The Beatles. As we unravel the threads that intertwine music, mysticism, and manipulation, we uncover a landscape where the esoteric forces of the occult intricately interweave with the fabric of popular culture.

The Beatles, hailed as the architects of the "British Invasion," not only revolutionized the music industry but also became cultural icons who shaped the zeitgeist of the 1960s. Their experimentation with unconventional musical styles, groundbreaking album concepts, and introspective lyrics positioned them as pioneers in the world of popular music. However, beneath the surface of their artistic evolution, a deeper current of intrigue emerges, rooted in esoteric exploration and occult symbolism.

It is within this context that we must consider Jimmy Savile's potential impact on The Beatles and, consequently, the wider UK pop music industry. Savile, himself alleged to have had occult connections and associations with secret societies, poignantly intersects with the band's trajectory, raising questions about the extent of his influence and manipulation within their artistic endeavors.

One aspect that warrants examination is the occult symbolism and spiritual themes that began to permeate The Beatles' work during their most experimental phase. Albums such as "Revolver," "Sgt. Pepper's Lonely Hearts Club Band," and "The White Album" showcase a departure from their earlier pop sensibilities, venturing into a realm of abstract soundscapes, intricate arrangements, and enigmatic lyrics. This artistic shift aligned with the broader cultural exploration of spirituality, Eastern philosophies, and mysticism that defined the era.

Savile's purported connections to occult circles and his alleged knowledge of esoteric practices invite speculation about his potential role in guiding The Beatles' artistic choices. Could he have acted as a conduit for occult wisdom, introducing the band to mystical concepts and symbolism that infused their music? The presence of Aleister Crowley's teachings, the figurehead of occultism in the 20th century, can be discerned not only in The Beatles' work but also in their personal lives, further deepening the enigma. Crowley's influence, rooted in Thelema and the exploration of personal will and spiritual transformation, may have resonated with Savile's alleged occult interests and become intertwined with The Beatles' creative processes.

Furthermore, the notion of Savile functioning as a facilitator of occult practices within the band's inner circle cannot be ignored. Allegations suggest that Savile's connections to secret societies and knowledge of esoteric rituals provided him with the tools to manipulate energetic forces and influence the lives of others. Considering this, we must contemplate the possibility that he introduced The Beatles to rituals, practices, or conceptual frameworks that nurtured their exploration of the mystical and occult. Such a hypothesis raises compelling questions about the extent to which Savile's influence infiltrated not only their music but also their personal lives and spiritual journeys.

Additionally, the impact of Savile's occult influences extends beyond The Beatles themselves and ripples into the broader UK pop music industry. The Beatles held a unique position as musical pioneers and cultural icons, with their art and artistic choices playing a pivotal role in shaping popular culture. As they forged paths and experimented with esoteric concepts and imagery, they undoubtedly influenced subsequent generations of musicians and artists.

Consider the pervasive influence of The Beatles' music and cultural impact on 1960s and beyond. The notions of counterculture, social revolution, and artistic innovation became inextricably intertwined with their artistic legacy. Savile's close association with The Beatles, coupled with his alleged occult interests, raises the question of whether his potential manipulative presence influenced the wider industry. Did his connections afford him the opportunity to subtly shape the trajectory of popular music, infusing it with occult symbolism, and introducing subtle themes of control and manipulation?

As we navigate the intricacies of Savile's alleged involvement and the occult symbiosis between his presence and The Beatles, we must remain vigilant in our search for truth. The potential long-term impact of his occult influences on the UK pop music industry occupies a space where the boundaries between artistic freedom, spiritual exploration, and potential manipulation become ethereal. By examining the nuances of this connection, we can begin to uncover the hidden tendrils that weave together music, magic, and the enigmatic presence of Jimmy Savile.

Analysis of the similarities between Savile and Count Dracula as "energy vampires"

In this section, we delve into the intriguing parallels between Jimmy Savile and the iconic character of Count Dracula, examining how both figures embody the concept of "energy vampires." We explore the notion that Savile, like the fictional Count, possessed an uncanny ability to feed off the energies of others, exerting control and manipulation for his own nefarious purposes.

Count Dracula, a creation of Bram Stoker's Gothic novel, epitomizes the archetype of the vampire – a creature that sustains itself by draining the life force of others. Dracula feeds on the vital energies of his victims, leaving them weakened and susceptible to his control. While Savile may not possess supernatural abilities, there are striking similarities between his modus operandi and the predatory nature of the vampire legend.

One of the defining characteristics of Jimmy Savile was his unmatched charisma and captivating presence. He effortlessly captivated those around him, drawing them into his sphere of influence. This ability to charm and manipulate resonates with the image of the vampire, who employs seduction and allure to ensnare their victims. Savile, like the vampire, possessed an undeniable magnetism that made it difficult for others to resist his overpowering influence.

Furthermore, much like the vampire who targets vulnerable individuals, Savile seemed to possess an uncanny knack for identifying and exploiting those who were in need or susceptible to his manipulative tactics. Whether it was the young and impressionable, the hopeful and ambitious, or the lonely and longing for connection, Savile had a seemingly innate understanding of human psychology, enabling him to prey upon the vulnerabilities of others.

Savile's involvement in charitable endeavors and philanthropic work played a significant part in his modus operandi. He positioned himself as a figure of benevolence, using his charity work to gain access to influential individuals and cultivate a public image of altruism. Yet, there is a darker undercurrent to examine – the possibility that his charitable actions were an elaborate façade, a means to extract the life energy, or "soul energy," from those he purported to help. This concept aligns with the vampire mythos, as they drain the life force of their victims to sustain their own existence.

Furthermore, the notion of energy manipulation and control can be further explored through the lens of Savile's alleged involvement with occult practices. Occult rituals often involve the harnessing and directing of subtle energies for various purposes. Savile's connections to occult circles, coupled with his charismatic persona, raise questions about whether he utilized these esoteric practices to gather and manipulate energy for personal gain. Just as the vampire draws sustenance from its victims, Savile may have sought to harness the energies of those around him to fuel his own ambitions and desires.

The parallel between Savile and the vampire archetype becomes even more intriguing when considering the alleged manipulation of ley lines. Ley lines, believed by some to be invisible energy pathways that crisscross the Earth, can be associated with locations of power or significance. Savile's presence and associations with places like Stoke Mandeville, Broadmoor, Duncroft, and Broadcasting House – potentially significant ley line sites – invite speculation about his potential manipulation of these subtle energetic forces. Similar to the vampire who harnesses the energy within their surroundings, Savile may have strategically positioned himself in locations where ley lines intersected, using them to amplify his own personal power and influence.

In conclusion, the parallels between Jimmy Savile and the character of Count Dracula, particularly as "energy vampires," provoke thought-provoking contemplation. Both figures possess charismatic allure, targeting the vulnerable for their own gain. The manipulation and control exerted by Savile, coupled with allegations of involvement in occult practices and potential manipulation of ley lines, lend credence to the notion that he, like the vampire, thrived on the life force of those around him.

By examining the striking similarities between Savile and the vampire archetype, we gain further insight into the darker aspects of his character and actions. The concept of the "energy vampire" serves as a lens through which we can begin to understand the mechanisms underlying Savile's insidious influence and manipulation, highlighting the extent to which he preyed on the energies of others for his own self-aggrandizement. Thus, we unravel a layer of the enigma that was Jimmy Savile and the potential occult forces that shaped his manipulative persona.

Chapter 7: Secret Societies and Royalty

In this chapter, we embark on a fascinating exploration into the potential connections between Jimmy Savile and secret societies, as well as the intricate interplay between occult practices, influential figures, and the enigmatic realm of royalty. As we delve into the depths of these hidden networks, we begin to unravel a web of intrigue that adds yet another layer of complexity to Savile's story.

Throughout history, secret societies have existed, operating behind closed doors and shrouded in mystery. These clandestine groups have been known to wield significant power and influence, working toward their hidden objectives and often exerting control over various aspects of society. It is within this context that we speculate on the possibility of Savile's involvement with such societies, unveiling the covert forces that may have shaped his actions and afforded him an unparalleled reach.

One cannot overlook the intriguing role that the British monarchy, with its long-standing traditions and deep historical roots, may have played in Savile's story. Royals have both influenced and been influenced by the occult throughout the ages, leading to questions about potential links between Savile and members of the royal family. Numerous renowned secret societies, such as the Freemasons, have historically boasted members within royal circles, raising the specter of hidden hands guiding seemingly unrelated events.

Of particular interest is the ambiguous gift bestowed upon Savile by none other than Prince Charles himself. The gift, consisting of cigars and a mysterious note, raises perplexing questions about the nature of their relationship and the true extent of Savile's connection to the royal family. Was Savile a trusted confidant, or did he simply possess a unique ability to navigate the intricate world of the elite? We delve deep into this enigmatic exchange, scrutinizing the possible occult significance of the gift and its role in Savile's overarching narrative.

Furthermore, the historical landscape reveals a rich tapestry of connections between secret services, occult practices, and influential figures. These connections have often led to whispers of covert operations, manipulation of power dynamics, and the utilization of occult rituals for personal and collective gain. With Savile's alleged involvement in secret societies and his proximity to influential circles, the mysteries surrounding his motivations and actions take on a whole new dimension.

It is worth mentioning that the occult and secret societies have long rooted themselves within the fabric of society, infiltrating institutions, and influencing the course of events from behind the scenes. From the ancient Egyptian priesthood to the medieval Templars, from the esoteric traditions of the Hermetic Order of the Golden Dawn to the infamous illuminati, secret societies have thrived on the fringes of societal knowledge, their actions and agendas often obscured from public view. By examining their historical significance and the potential linkages to Jimmy Savile, we peer through the veil, seeking to unravel hidden machinations and comprehend the extent to which occult practices may have influenced his trajectory.

By understanding the intricate relationships between secret societies, influential figures, and the occult, we aim to shed light on the motivations behind Savile's actions – motivations that may reach far beyond the criminal acts for which he has become infamous. We must question whether his involvement in secret societies provided him with the tools and resources necessary to manipulate the very fabric of society, making him a puppet master pulling strings from the shadows.

In conclusion, this chapter delves into the labyrinthine connections between Jimmy Savile, secret societies, and the world of royalty. By peering behind the cloak of secrecy and examining historical precedents, we inch closer to unraveling the true nature of Savile's influence and the occult forces at play. With each revelation, the enigma surrounding Savile deepens, leaving us with more profound questions and a sense that there is still much more to uncover in our quest to unmask his occult secrets.

Exploration of Jimmy Savile's potential affiliations with secret societies

In this section, we embark on a fascinating exploration into Jimmy Savile's potential affiliations with secret societies, peering through the veil of secrecy to unearth connections that may shed light on the enigmatic nature of his actions and motivations. While concrete evidence linking Savile to specific secret societies may be elusive, a careful analysis of his life and associations reveals intriguing patterns that invite speculation and further investigation.

Throughout history, secret societies have operated in the shadows, utilizing rituals, symbols, and clandestine networks to exert influence and shape the course of events. These organizations, often cloaked in mystery, have been known to draw individuals from diverse backgrounds while serving as platforms for shared ideologies, hidden agendas, and the preservation of esoteric knowledge. It is within this context that we explore the potential involvement of Jimmy Savile in these enigmatic groups.

Savile's close connections with influential figures from various fields serve as primary sources of intrigue and potential ties to secret societies. His ability to effortlessly navigate across different social strata enabled him to establish relationships with politicians, royalty, entertainers, and even members of the clergy. While these associations might be perceived as merely the result of his charismatic personality and high-profile position in the entertainment industry, they also raise questions about the extent of his behind-the-scenes involvement in secret societies.

One such secretive organization that has been the subject of speculation regarding Savile's possible affiliation is the Freemasons. With a history stretching back centuries, the Freemasons have both been revered and vilified, their rituals and symbolism inspiring curiosity and conspiracy theories alike. Given the nature of their secretive practices and the tendency to shield their inner workings from public view, it is challenging to definitively ascertain Savile's involvement with this influential fraternity. However, the affinity between the fraternity's values and Savile's inclination towards charity work and public service raises intriguing parallels, increasing the likelihood of some form of association.

Another avenue of exploration lies in the potential connections between Savile and Thelema, an esoteric religious philosophy founded by the notorious occultist Aleister Crowley. Crowley, whose influence seeped into the counterculture movements of the 1960s, was known for his controversial beliefs and practices. Thelema, with its emphasis on individualism, spiritual exploration, and the manipulation of reality through magical means, may have resonated with certain facets of Savile's enigmatic persona. While Savile himself may not have publicly espoused Thelemic ideologies, the historical overlap between Crowley's teachings and the countercultural zeitgeist of the time makes it worth investigating potential links between the two figures.

Examining Savile's affiliations with knighted orders, such as the Knights of Malta, Knights of St. Gregory, and his appointment as a Knight of the Realm, adds another layer of intrigue to his potential involvement with secret societies. These prestigious titles, bestowed upon him in recognition of his charitable work and contribution to society, invite speculation on whether they also served as indicators of membership or honorary roles within esoteric circles.

However, it is important to approach these explorations with a discerning eye, recognizing that speculation surrounding secret societies often breeds misinformation and sensationalism. While the potential affiliations discussed in this chapter present compelling possibilities, further research and evidence are necessary to substantiate any claims definitively.

In conclusion, this section explores the potential affiliations of Jimmy Savile with secret societies, building on the patterns that emerge from his associations with influential figures and his involvement in charitable activities. By delving into the historical context and esoteric traditions associated with secretive organizations, we strive to unravel the enigma surrounding Savile's motivations and actions, leaving open the possibility that hidden forces, guided by the principles of secret societies, played a role in shaping his trajectory.

Analysis of the connections between secret services, royalty, and occult practices in history

Within the intricate tapestry of historical events, numerous connections have been observed linking secret services, royalty, and occult practices. This section delves into the rich history that underscores these connections, shedding light on the potential implications they may have had in relation to Jimmy Savile and his enigmatic role within this intricate web.

Throughout centuries, secret services have played a pivotal role in safeguarding the interests of nations, often operating covertly to gather intelligence, protect national security, and, at times, exert influence on a global scale. Their clandestine nature has allowed them to operate in the shadows, away from the prying eyes of the public. Yet, this cloak of secrecy has also fueled speculation about their involvement in arcane practices and their dealings with occult knowledge.

The close association between secret services and elements of the occult can be traced back to various periods in history. One particularly intriguing chapter lies in the activities of the Hermetic Order of the Golden Dawn, an organization that sought to explore magical and mystical teachings. Its founder, Samuel Liddell MacGregor Mathers, was known to have had connections with intelligence services. This alignment between esoteric knowledge and intelligence work raises questions about whether similar intertwined dynamics existed in other secret societies of the era.

In examining these connections, it becomes apparent that members of royalty, too, have been drawn into this enigmatic realm. Throughout history, monarchs and nobility have been linked with the occult, cementing their authority and seeking to harness hidden forces for personal gain or to shape the destiny of nations. From the alleged dealings of Queen Elizabeth I with Elizabethan magician John Dee to the intrigue surrounding the interaction between King Louis XVI and the occultist Count Cagliostro, the historical footprints of secret societies within royal courts are undeniable.

The British monarchy, with its centuries-spanning legacy, has not escaped the influence of the occult. Rumors and tales of royal involvements in arcane practices have swirled throughout the ages, fuelling the imagination and leading to speculation about hidden agendas. Secret societies, such as the Freemasons, have frequently boasted members from royal circles, creating an environment in which esoteric practices can interweave with political intrigue and influence.

This historical context sets the stage for contemplating the potential linkages between Jimmy Savile and occult practices within royal circles. Savile's close proximity to influential figures, including the royal family, invites speculation about the extent to which he may have been privy to occult knowledge or occult-influenced activities. Some theorists posit that these connections might have facilitated his rise to prominence and afforded him a level of influence that extended beyond the realm of entertainment and charity.

Furthermore, the complexities surrounding Savile's association with Prince Charles and the disputed significance of the cigars and note gifted to him offer fertile ground for exploration.

Many have pondered the hidden meanings behind this exchange, questioning whether it symbolizes a deeper connection rarely unveiled to the public eye. The potential convergence of Prince Charles' royal lineage, his position within the British monarchy, and the secretive world of occult symbolism adds another layer of intrigue to the narrative surrounding Savile.

It is essential to approach the examination of these connections with a discerning eye, balancing historical patterns and anecdotal evidence with the need for concrete proof. Nevertheless, the entanglement between secret services, royalty, and occult practices throughout history cannot be ignored. Indeed, it serves as an invitation to further scrutinize the motivations and potential behind Savile's actions, shedding light on the existence and influence of hidden forces that operate beyond the knowledge of the public.

In conclusion, this section provides an in-depth analysis of the connections between secret services, royalty, and occult practices throughout history. Drawing on historical precedents and the intertwining dynamics of power, it invites speculation regarding the potential implications of these connections in relation to Jimmy Savile. By shedding light on the historical context, we develop a framework for further investigation into the hidden forces that may have shaped Savile's actions and the enigmatic web in which he operated.

Examination of Prince Charles' ambiguous gift and note to Savile and its potential significance

One of the most puzzling aspects in the intricate web of connections surrounding Jimmy Savile lies in the ambiguous gift and note bestowed upon him by none other than Prince Charles, heir to the British throne. This section dives deep into the enigma surrounding this exchange, analyzing its potential occult significance and the broader implications it raises.

The exchange between Savile and Prince Charles, documented through a gift of cigars and a mysterious note, has long sparked speculation, evoking countless theories and conjectures about the nature of their relationship. Exchanging gifts can often serve as symbolic acts, carrying hidden meanings and conveying sentiments that go beyond the surface gesture. In the case of Savile, whose life contains a plethora of hidden symbols and ambiguous connections, the circumstances surrounding this exchange introduce another layer of intrigue.

The nature of the gift itself, cigars, adds another dimension to the puzzle. Throughout history, cigars have been associated with rituals, celebrations, and even secret societies. The act of smoking has been intertwined with spiritual practices, symbolizing a conduit between the material and spiritual realms, and serving as a vehicle to release or harness unseen energies. While it is crucial not to attribute undue importance to a straightforward act of gift-giving, the inclusion of cigars in this exchange cannot be overlooked.

Equally fascinating is the note accompanying the gift. Unfortunately, the contents and precise wording of this note remain elusive, leaving room for speculation and interpretation. However, even without definitive knowledge of the exact words written on the note, it is the very existence of this mysterious correspondence that fuels curiosity and invites deeper analysis. The concealed message within these written words carries potential hidden meanings, open to exploration through the lens of occult symbolism and the nuanced language used by those familiar with esoteric practices.

To fully comprehend the potential significance of this exchange, it is important to consider the historical context of occult practices within royal circles. The British monarchy has long maintained a connection to esoteric traditions and secret societies, often veiling their involvement through symbols and rituals. Freemasonry, for instance, has historically attracted members from within royal circles, strengthening the ties between royalty and secret societies. Thus, the connection between Savile, a prominent figure with alleged associations with occult practices, and Prince Charles, a member of the royal family, opens up the possibility of hidden forces at work.

The speculative nature of this analysis should not diminish the potential implications that arise from the intersection of occult symbolism, royal connections, and the presence of secretive networks. It further underscores the importance of scrutinizing the motivations and actions of individuals who operate within these spheres. When examining Savile's mysterious gift and note from Prince Charles through this lens, we begin to consider the hidden layers of influence and hidden agendas that may exist, extending beyond the public image and overt affiliations.

It is important to emphasize the need for caution and a rigorous approach to avoid falling into the trap of baseless conspiracy theories. While speculation may invite imaginative connections, it is vital to seek substantial evidence and corroborating factors to support any conclusions drawn. Nevertheless, the existence of this peculiar exchange between Savile and Prince Charles carries weight, prompting us to question the broader significance it may hold in the complex narrative surrounding Savile's hidden associations and potential for involvement in occult activities.

In conclusion, this section explores in detail the ambiguous nature of the gift and note exchanged between Jimmy Savile and Prince Charles. By delving into the potential occult symbolism of cigars and contemplating the underlying significance of the mysterious note within the context of royal connections and secretive networks, we uncover new dimensions in the enigmatic web enveloping Savile's life. These cryptic exchanges open doors to further examination, as we strive to understand the true motivations, hidden forces, and potential occult influences that shaped Savile's actions and extended his reach beyond the realm of public acclaim.

Chapter 8: The Dualistic Nature of Magic

In this thought-provoking chapter, we immerse ourselves in the complex and paradoxical realm of magic – a world of limitless possibilities, where light and darkness intertwine to shape the very fabric of reality. We unveil the dualistic nature of magic and delve into the intriguing notion that Jimmy Savile may have embraced both the white and black arts, employing their powers to further his hidden agenda.

To comprehend the intricacies of this duality, we must first acknowledge the long-standing belief in the existence of two distinct forces within the magical arts – the benevolent and malevolent. These contrasting aspects have permeated numerous mythologies, religions, and esoteric traditions throughout history, encapsulating the concept of light and dark, good and evil, creation and destruction.

As we embark on our exploration, we observe that the magical practices undertaken by individuals such as Savile often transcend the simplistic dichotomy of good and evil, leading us to question the true intentions behind their actions. It is here where we tread the shadowy line between white and black magic with caution, seeking to understand whether Savile employed both sides in his pursuit of power and control.

In the study of the occult, white magic is often associated with benevolent actions, healing, protection, and the manifestation of positive intentions. Practitioners of this path traditionally seek to align themselves with the higher principles of love, compassion, and altruism, utilizing magical rituals and practices for the betterment of oneself and others. In this regard, we explore the possibility that certain aspects of Savile's philanthropic endeavors and his public persona may have been a guise for engaging in benevolent magical acts.

Conversely, black magic conjures images of malevolence, hexes, curses, and the manipulation of energies for personal gain or harm. Embedded within this realm are the controversial practices of manipulation, control, and the pursuit of power at any cost. While black magic has long been stigmatized as inherently evil, we approach it with a balanced perspective, striving to comprehend if Savile may have delved into these obscure arts to fulfill his hidden desires and exert control over others.

Amidst our exploration, we must not overlook the influence of the occultist Alastair Crowley, a notorious figure who embraced both the light and dark aspects of magic. Savile's alleged connections to Crowley, including their shared interests in Thelema, an esoteric philosophy, raise intriguing questions. We shall uncover the potential significance of these connections, piecing together the puzzle of Savile's occult leanings and his possible parallel with Crowley's ideology.

Furthermore, we investigate the potential motivations behind Savile's adoption of both white and black magical practices. Could his involvement in benevolent acts have been a means to accumulate positive energies, to balance the karmic scales and gain favor with influential figures or unseen forces? Conversely, we ponder if his foray into the dark arts allowed him to manipulate subtle energies, bend the will of others, or even engage in rituals that fed his desire for power and control.

To amplify our understanding, we assess the enigmatic relationship between Savile and the concept of energy vampirism – a notion where individuals feed off the energies of others for their personal gain. Drawing comparisons to the legends of Count Dracula, who thrived by draining the life force of their victims, we delve into the realm of energetic manipulation. In this light, we contemplate whether Savile's charismatic presence and ability to captivate others masked his true intentions as he sought to extract and harness the vital energies that emanated from those under his influence.

Amidst the shadows of Savile's intricate life, we encounter whispers of secret society affiliations, which further blur the lines between white and black magic. Within the hidden folds of secret orders, esoteric societies, and ancient traditions lie ancient wisdom, arcane practices, and the covert wielding of magical power. We examine the potential convergence of Savile's involvement in such circles, exploring how these affiliations may have influenced his adoption and mastery of both benevolent and malevolent arts.

In conclusion, this chapter unfurls before us a fascinating exploration of the dualistic nature of magic within the context of Jimmy Savile's enigmatic existence. Our investigation traverses the boundaries of right and wrong, benevolence and malevolence, uncovering the possibility that he treaded the fine line between these opposing forces. As we peel back the layers of his occult leanings, we come ever closer to comprehending the motivations behind his actions, the mechanisms of his influence, and the extent to which magic played a role in shaping his dark arts.

Discussion on the Two Sides of Magic

In this section, we plunge into a comprehensive analysis of the dualistic nature of magic - a profound interplay between opposing forces that shape the very fabric of mystical realms. By exploring the intricacies of white and black magic, we seek to unravel the extent to which Jimmy Savile may have embraced both aspects, plunging into the depths of arcane practices to further his hidden agenda.

At the heart of this exploration lies the concept of white magic, often associated with benevolent intentions, healing, protection, and the manifestation of positive outcomes. Practitioners of the white arts are driven by a noble pursuit of spiritual growth, harmony, and the well-being of oneself and others. Such magical rituals are believed to tap into the higher cosmic forces, aligning with concepts such as love, compassion, and altruism.

Within the context of Jimmy Savile's enigmatic existence, we scrutinize his philanthropic endeavors and the public persona he meticulously crafted. It is here that we seek to discern if his acts of charity and selflessness were manifestations of white magic, a guise employed to channel positive energies and project an image of goodness. Could his relentless fundraising efforts, involvement with hospitals, and fostering relationships with charitable organizations have been motivated by a genuine desire to serve and uplift humanity? Or did Savile cleverly exploit the inherent power of white magic to consolidate his influence and control over others?

While the light side of magic draws us into realms of benevolence, the shadows beckon us towards black magic – a realm shrouded in its own mystique of forbidden knowledge, manipulation, and personal gain. Black magic is often associated with the use of dark arts to manifest selfish desires, inflict harm upon others, or bend the will of the unsuspecting. The practice of black magic throughout history has been both feared and condemned, accompanied by tales of curses, hexes, and malevolence.

In our journey to uncover the darker shades of Savile's occult leanings, we explore if he dabbled in the forbidden arts associated with black magic. Were there hidden rituals, talismans, or occult practices that he engaged in to manipulate subtle energies and exert control over others? It is pertinent to contemplate whether the very act of wielding black magic enabled him to enforce his influence, fulfilling his deepest desires while potentially perpetrating harm upon those who crossed his path.

An essential aspect of our discussion pertains to the motivations behind Savile's engagement with both white and black magic. Could his involvement in benevolent acts have been a calculated means to accumulate positive energies, balancing the karmic scales while simultaneously gaining favor with influential figures or unseen forces? We probe the depths of his psyche, questioning if Savile deliberately sought the acquisition of beneficial energies for his own purposes, harnessing them to amplify his charismatic aura and advance his hidden ambitions.

As we navigate the labyrinthine undercurrents of Savile's occult connections, we encounter the mysterious world of secret societies. These clandestine organizations, steeped in ancient wisdom and arcane practices, have long been associated with the convergence of both white and black magical arts. We scrutinize potential affiliations Savile may have had with these secret orders, assessing the impact they had on his mastery of opposing forces within the magical realm.

It is vital to address the ethical implications inherent in the pursuit and usage of both white and black magic. Moral debates surrounding these practices have persisted across cultures, histories, and belief systems. As we confront Savile's ambiguous journey, we shed light on the ethical quandaries that emerge, delicately acknowledging the thin line that separates the pursuit of knowledge, power, and personal desires from the potential infliction of harm.

In conclusion, the exploration of the dualistic nature of magic reveals a multifaceted aspect of Jimmy Savile's enigma. His alleged immersion in both white and black magical arts unveils a complex tapestry woven with benevolence, control, and manipulation. By dissecting his motivations and delving into the depths of occult influences, we inch closer to unraveling the enigmatic persona that lurked beneath the charismatic veneer. Our analysis unearths profound questions about the intentions, desires, and extent to which Savile wielded the opposing forces within the magical realm, leaving us to ponder the complex interplay of light and dark that informed his actions.

Analysis of his potential involvement in both benevolent and malevolent practices

As we explore the dualistic nature of magic in relation to Jimmy Savile, we begin to unravel the intricate web of his potential involvement in both benevolent and malevolent practices. To fully comprehend the depths of this duality, we must first acknowledge that magic, like any other human endeavor, encompasses a vast spectrum of intentions and outcomes.

In considering Savile's alleged connection to the occult, we encounter a perplexing conundrum. On one hand, we have the image of Savile as a philanthropist, dedicating his time and resources to numerous charitable causes. The sheer magnitude of his charitable work, with its immense impact on hospitals, children's organizations, and various institutions, is undeniable. He fostered relationships with important figures in the charity sector, using his fame and charisma to rally support and generate donations. This benevolent side of Savile casts him as a noble figure, channeling his energy and influence towards the betterment of society.

However, it is precisely within this noble facade that the duality of Savile's potential involvement in the dark arts comes to light. Throughout history, the concept of performative philanthropy has been linked to the channeling of sinister energies or the manipulation of unsuspecting victims. Interestingly, Savile's extensive charitable work raises questions about the true motivations behind his actions. Could it be that, hidden beneath the veil of virtuous deeds, lurked a cunning energy manipulator, harnessing the goodwill of others for his own purposes?

To fathom the depth of this duality, we must acknowledge the ancient belief in the balancing of karma – the notion that one must counterbalance negative actions with positive ones to achieve spiritual equilibrium. The charitable acts performed by Savile, such as his marathon runs and tireless fundraising efforts, might be seen as an attempt to balance his potential involvement in the dark arts – a calculated effort to redeem himself in some cosmic ledger. This manipulation of karma through philanthropy, known as "greenwashing" in occult circles, exists as a plausible explanation for the paradoxical nature of his actions.

Furthermore, the concept of "soul energy" takes center stage when examining Savile's duality. Within occult principles, it is believed that one can harvest and accumulate energy from various sources, including human interactions, emotions, and acts of kindness. Savile's charismatic persona, his charm, and his ability to connect with people from all walks of life may have served as a means to gather this potent energy. By engaging with the public, across the wide range of his television appearances and charitable endeavors, he strategically cultivated a following that would unknowingly provide him with a vein of soul energy to tap into for his own occult purposes.

It is imperative to underscore that the dualistic nature of magic extends beyond the individual, infiltrating societal structures and power dynamics. Investigating the occult influence within Savile's actions reveals the potential involvement of hidden forces, secret societies, and influential figures who may have played a role in his trajectory. The occult, with its secret societies and covert practices, has long been associated with manipulation, deceit, and the acquisition of power.

By traversing the intricate landscape of magic's duality in relation to Savile, we confront a myriad of questions. Was his seemingly benevolent facade merely a means to access hidden energies and manipulate subtle forces for his own gain? Could his extensive charity work have been a calculated ploy to gather soul energy, ultimately fueling his own personal and arcane ambitions? Were his actions a deliberate orchestration to balance the equilibrium of karma, an attempt to compensate for darker deeds?

It is within the exploration of these puzzling inquiries that we begin to untangle the true motivations behind Savile's involvement in both benevolent and malevolent practices. As we progress further into the secrets of his occult connections and the influences that shaped his actions, we find ourselves on the precipice of a revelation that may shed light on the enigmatic duality that lies at the heart of Jimmy Savile's occult journey.

Exploration of the motivations behind his actions and the expanse of his influence

Having traversed the complex terrain of Jimmy Savile's alleged involvement in both benevolent and malevolent practices, we now turn our attention to the motivations that may have driven his enigmatic actions. Furthermore, we venture into untrodden territory, seeking to grasp the true expanse of his influence and the far-reaching implications of his occult pursuits.

To unravel the motivations that propelled Savile into the realm of the dark arts, we must delve into the depths of his psyche and explore the intricate interplay between power, control, and personal gratification. Savile, like many individuals drawn to the occult, may have possessed an insatiable hunger for power, seeking to manipulate the energies around him to satisfy his desires and fulfill his ambitions. Whether driven by a thirst for control, a craving for recognition, or a yearning for immortality, these motivations often serve as catalysts for individuals to delve into the forbidden realms of the occult.

Examining Savile's vast web of connections, we find ourselves confronted with a tapestry interwoven with influential figures from the realms of politics, royalty, and entertainment. Such extensive associations raise questions about the true extent of his influence and the possible collusion among those in positions of power. As we journey through the corridors of influence and secret societies, we confront the tantalizing prospect that Savile's reach extended far beyond the realm of his public persona. It is plausible that he was merely a pawn in a grander game orchestrated by shadowy forces, utilizing his charm and charismatic allure to further their own agendas.

Moreover, we must consider the intricacies of Savile's affiliation with secret societies, which have historically acted as breeding grounds for occult practices and manipulation of esoteric knowledge. His membership in the ranks of the Knights of Malta, the Knights Commander of St. Gregory, and the Knights of the Realm hints at a deeper involvement in the workings of secretive organizations. The mingling of occult symbolism and rituals within these societies raises suspicions about the potential influence they may have had on Savile's actions and the shaping of his occult persona.

Another aspect that demands scrutiny is the ambiguous gift and note bestowed upon Savile by none other than Prince Charles, a figure renowned for his keen interest in environmentalism, alternative medicine, and esoteric philosophies. Speculation abounds regarding the true meaning behind this exchange, with some suggesting that it may have represented a covert message or acknowledgment of shared beliefs. Whether this connection can be attributed to a shared interest in the occult or an innocent exchange between acquaintances, it adds to the tapestry of intrigue surrounding Savile's occult leanings.

As we move deeper into the occult undercurrents of Savile's life, it becomes evident that his actions may not have been confined to personal gratification and the wielding of power. The occult, throughout history, has served as a vehicle for influencing societal structures and shaping the collective consciousness. With Savile's reach extending across the realms of entertainment, charity, and public engagement, questions arise regarding the true extent of his occult influence on the psyches of the masses.

The manipulation of ley lines, known for their subtle and invisible energies, enters the equation as we probe the depths of Savile's potential grasp over occult forces. Locations associated with his activities, such as Stoke Mandeville, Broadmoor, Duncroft, and Broadcasting House, take on a newfound significance when viewed through the lens of ley line manipulation. Could it be that Savile strategically leveraged these specific locations, aligning them with his occult intentions to amplify his influence, gather energies, or even perform clandestine rituals?

Ultimately, the exploration of the motivations behind Savile's actions and the expanse of his occult influence raises profound questions. Was he driven solely by personal ambition, seeking power and control through his involvement in both benevolent and malevolent practices? Or was he part of a much larger network, a cog in a sinister machine that sought to manipulate societal structures and harness the occult forces for their own hidden agendas?

In the pursuit of truth, we must unravel the complex web of motivations driving Savile's occult pursuits while considering the far-reaching ramifications of his actions. By daring to confront the shadows that cast doubt and uncertainty, we may unearth a deeper understanding of the enigmatic figure that is Jimmy Savile and the dark arts that characterized his tumultuous existence.

Chapter 9: Charitable Work and Manipulation

In this pivotal chapter, we unveil a fascinating aspect of Jimmy Savile's life that has long been regarded as a beacon of his apparent goodness – his extensive charitable work. With a flamboyant public persona that seemingly overflowed with kindness and generosity, Savile's philanthropic endeavors were celebrated and admired by the masses. Yet, we must pause and question the underlying motivations behind his charity, raising the possibility that it served as a strategically crafted facade to mask a much darker agenda.

To comprehend the intricate interplay between Savile's charitable work and the manipulation he purportedly engaged in, we must first examine the breadth and depth of his philanthropic reach. Savile's involvement in charitable endeavors spanned a wide spectrum, ranging from local community initiatives to large-scale national campaigns. He tirelessly campaigned and fundraised for a myriad of causes, particularly focusing on healthcare institutions, including hospitals and hospices. His self-proclaimed role as a "fixer" further accentuated his dedication to making the wishes of others come true, particularly children, through his iconic television program "Jim'll Fix It."

One cannot dispute the sheer volume of funds Savile raised for charitable causes, amounting to millions of pounds over the years. The substantial financial contributions he facilitated would have undoubtedly made a significant impact on countless individuals and organizations. However, as we delve deeper into his charitable work, a disconcerting pattern emerges – one that raises questions about the underlying motives behind Savile's seemingly altruistic actions.

As we explore the concept of manipulation, it becomes apparent that Savile's philanthropy served as a powerful tool for shaping public perception and garnering influence. Through his charitable endeavors, he actively cultivated relationships with influential figures, including politicians, members of the royal family, and other high-ranking individuals. By aligning himself with the corridors of power, Savile positioned himself strategically to access channels of authority and further solidify his influential network.

The question arises: How did Savile utilize his charity work to manipulate and control those around him? One theory suggests that he harnessed the concept of karma to his advantage. By engaging in altruistic acts and channeling positive energy through his charity work, Savile may have sought to balance out the negative energy created by his covert actions. This manipulation of karma allowed him to continue his nefarious activities while maintaining a perceived positive public image – a mask that shielded him from suspicion for decades.

Moreover, we must explore the concept of "soul energy" and how Savile potentially sought to harness it through his charitable endeavors. According to esoteric theories, every action, thought, and emotion generates energy that can be harnessed and manipulated. Savile's extensive interaction with diverse individuals within his charitable network provided him with a vast reservoir of soul energy. This energetic currency, collected via his public persona, may have granted him direct access to influential individuals and opened doors that would have otherwise remained closed.

To further complicate matters, we must examine the possible connection between Savile's charitable work and the manipulation of subtle forces – namely, the utilization of ley lines locations. Ley lines, long believed to be invisible channels of energy that crisscross the Earth's surface, have been linked to mystical and paranormal phenomena. It is intriguing to note that some of Savile's charitable endeavors were situated in locations reputed to intersect these energetic pathways. From Stoke Mandeville, where he played a significant role in the development of the Spinal Injuries Center, to Broadmoor, where he acted as a "volunteer porter" at the high-security psychiatric hospital, these sites draw attention to a potentially significant deeper purpose to Savile's choices.

By positioning himself at these locations, energetically charged by the convergence of ley lines, Savile may have tapped into the subtler forces that permeate our world. Through his understanding, whether conscious or instinctual, of these unseen energies, he could have manipulated and directed them to his advantage, further enhancing his systemic control over individuals, institutions, and even society at large.

In conclusion, chapter nine delves into the intricate web woven between Jimmy Savile's philanthropy and his alleged manipulation of others. By examining the broad scope of his charitable work, we identify the patterns of influence and strategic positioning employed by Savile to secure his hold on power. We also explore the potential intertwining of karma, soul energy, and ley lines – concepts that shed light on the hidden machinations behind his public image. Join us on this fascinating journey as we unveil the dark underbelly of Jimmy Savile's charitable work, peeling back the layers to expose the potential sinister intentions that lurked beneath the veneer of goodness.

Chapter 9: Charitable Work and Manipulation

In this pivotal chapter, we unveil a fascinating aspect of Jimmy Savile's life that has long been regarded as a beacon of his apparent goodness – his extensive charitable work. With a flamboyant public persona that seemingly overflowed with kindness and generosity, Savile's philanthropic endeavors were celebrated and admired by the masses. Yet, we must pause and question the underlying motivations behind his charity, raising the possibility that it served as a strategically crafted facade to mask a much darker agenda.

To comprehend the intricate interplay between Savile's charitable work and the manipulation he purportedly engaged in, we must first examine the breadth and depth of his philanthropic reach. Savile's involvement in charitable endeavors spanned a wide spectrum, ranging from local community initiatives to large-scale national campaigns. He tirelessly campaigned and fundraised for a myriad of causes, particularly focusing on healthcare institutions, including hospitals and hospices. His self-proclaimed role as a "fixer" further accentuated his dedication to making the wishes of others come true, particularly children, through his iconic television program "Jim'll Fix It."

One cannot dispute the sheer volume of funds Savile raised for charitable causes, amounting to millions of pounds over the years. The substantial financial contributions he facilitated would have undoubtedly made a significant impact on countless individuals and organizations. However, as we delve deeper into his charitable work, a disconcerting pattern emerges – one that raises questions about the underlying motives behind Savile's seemingly altruistic actions.

As we explore the concept of manipulation, it becomes apparent that Savile's philanthropy served as a powerful tool for shaping public perception and garnering influence. Through his charitable endeavors, he actively cultivated relationships with influential figures, including politicians, members of the royal family, and other high-ranking individuals. By aligning himself with the corridors of power, Savile positioned himself strategically to access channels of authority and further solidify his influential network.

The question arises: How did Savile utilize his charity work to manipulate and control those around him? One theory suggests that he harnessed the concept of karma to his advantage. By engaging in altruistic acts and channeling positive energy through his charity work, Savile may have sought to balance out the negative energy created by his covert actions. This manipulation of karma allowed him to continue his nefarious activities while maintaining a perceived positive public image – a mask that shielded him from suspicion for decades.

Moreover, we must explore the concept of "soul energy" and how Savile potentially sought to harness it through his charitable endeavors. According to esoteric theories, every action, thought, and emotion generates energy that can be harnessed and manipulated. Savile's extensive interaction with diverse individuals within his charitable network provided him with a vast reservoir of soul energy. This energetic currency, collected via his public persona, may have granted him direct access to influential individuals and opened doors that would have otherwise remained closed.

To further complicate matters, we must examine the possible connection between Savile's charitable work and the manipulation of subtle forces – namely, the utilization of ley lines locations. Ley lines, long believed to be invisible channels of energy that crisscross the Earth's surface, have been linked to mystical and paranormal phenomena. It is intriguing to note that some of Savile's charitable endeavors were situated in locations reputed to intersect these energetic pathways. From Stoke Mandeville, where he played a significant role in the development of the Spinal Injuries Center, to Broadmoor, where he acted as a "volunteer porter" at the high-security psychiatric hospital, these sites draw attention to a potentially significant deeper purpose to Savile's choices.

By positioning himself at these locations, energetically charged by the convergence of ley lines, Savile may have tapped into the subtler forces that permeate our world. Through his understanding, whether conscious or instinctual, of these unseen energies, he could have manipulated and directed them to his advantage, further enhancing his systemic control over individuals, institutions, and even society at large.

In conclusion, chapter nine delves into the intricate web woven between Jimmy Savile's philanthropy and his alleged manipulation of others. By examining the broad scope of his charitable work, we identify the patterns of influence and strategic positioning employed by Savile to secure his hold on power. We also explore the potential intertwining of karma, soul energy, and ley lines – concepts that shed light on the hidden machinations behind his public image. Join us on this fascinating journey as we unveil the dark underbelly of Jimmy Savile's charitable work, peeling back the layers to expose the potential sinister intentions that lurked beneath the veneer of goodness.

Examination of Jimmy Savile's charitable work and its potential hidden motives

In this section, we embark on a detailed exploration of Jimmy Savile's extensive charitable work, shining a spotlight on the intricacies and potential hidden motives behind his seemingly selfless endeavors. While many hailed him as a beacon of goodness and generosity, we shall delve deeper to unravel the complex tapestry woven by Savile, raising questions about the ulterior motives that may have fueled his philanthropy.

One cannot dispute the astonishing magnitude of Savile's charitable efforts. His commitment to fundraising and supporting various causes was unparalleled, spanning a wide array of organizations, initiatives, and endeavors. Hospitals became a focal point of his benevolent focus, with his name becoming synonymous with institutions such as Stoke Mandeville, Leeds General Infirmary, and Broadmoor. Through his tireless advocacy, he channeled vast sums of money towards these medical establishments, contributing to the improvement of patient care and facilities.

While it is essential to acknowledge the positive impact of Savile's charitable work on the lives of many, it is equally important to examine the nuances that raise suspicions regarding underlying motives. One such aspect is the extent of Savile's involvement in the charities he supported. Unlike many philanthropists who choose to make financial contributions anonymously or through established foundations, Savile was front and center, actively participating in events, engaging directly with beneficiaries, and using his personal charisma to rally public support.

This active involvement begs the question: Was Savile driven purely by compassion and a genuine desire to make a difference, or was there an ulterior motive? Some speculate that Savile's charity work functioned as a smokescreen, meticulously crafted to deflect attention from his clandestine activities. By occupying the public eye as a tireless advocate for the vulnerable and downtrodden, he created a mythical shield that protected him from scrutiny for decades, enabling him to continue his exploitative actions undetected.

Furthermore, the sheer scale of Savile's charity work had a profound impact on his social standing and public perception. The high-profile nature of his philanthropy propelled him into the ranks of esteemed fundraisers, positioning him as one of the most prolific contributors in British history. However, we must ask ourselves whether this relentless pursuit of charity was primarily driven by benevolence or whether it served as ammunition in a calculated quest for power and influence. By positioning himself as a prominent philanthropist, Savile gained access to powerful individuals, including politicians and members of the royal family, forging connections that fortified his web of influence.

It is crucial to highlight the potential role of manipulation within Savile's charitable work. Utilizing his charismatic personality and intricate understanding of human psychology, he skillfully connected with people from all walks of life, winning their trust with a beguiling charisma that was hard to resist. This manipulation may have extended beyond mere social interaction, as he actively exploited the vulnerability and gratitude of those directly benefiting from his philanthropy. By bestowing favors, wish fulfilment, or granting access to exclusive events, Savile engendered a sense of indebtedness within his recipients, further tightening the grip of his influence.

Moreover, the concept of karma plays a significant role in understanding the potential hidden motives behind Savile's charitable work. To maintain the facade of a virtuous persona, he juxtaposed his malevolent deeds with acts of apparent selflessness – a strategy aimed at balancing the scales of karma. By engaging in philanthropy, he may have sought to counterbalance the negative energy generated by his nefarious activities, thus attaining a semblance of moral equilibrium. This manipulation of karma allowed him to continue his exploitations under the cover of charity, effectively shielding himself from suspicion for an extended period.

One cannot ignore the potential impact of the "soul energy" harvested through his charitable work. According to esoteric beliefs, every action, thought, and emotion generates energy that can be utilized or manipulated. Savile's extensive interaction with diverse individuals within his charitable network provided him with a vast reservoir of such soul energy. With every heartfelt act of gratitude, every display of adoration and appreciation, he potentially gained a form of energetic currency that could be redirected to his advantage. This energetic transaction granted him direct access to influential individuals and opened doors that would have otherwise remained closed.

In conclusion, section 9.1 delves into the multifaceted nature of Jimmy Savile's charitable work, fostering a deeper understanding of the potential hidden motives that fueled his seemingly altruistic endeavors. By examining the extensive reach of his philanthropy, we uncover the complex interplay between genuine compassion and manipulation for personal gain. The strategic positioning of himself within charity circles, the use of charisma and psychological tactics, the balance of karma, and the potential manipulation of soul energy all raise intricate questions about Savile's motivations and serve as a lens to decipher his hidden agenda. Join us as we peel back the layers of philanthropy to reveal the concealed underbelly of Jimmy Savile's actions.

Analysis of how his charity work may have served as a means to balance karma and gain access to influential figures

In this section, we embark on a comprehensive analysis of how Jimmy Savile's extensive charity work may have served as a means to balance karma and grant him access to influential individuals. By delving into the intricate web of motivations behind his philanthropic endeavors, we uncover a complex interplay between benevolence, manipulation, and the desire for personal gain.

To understand the potential role of karma in Savile's charity work, we must first explore the underlying principles of this ancient concept. Karma, with its roots in Eastern philosophies, posits that every action, thought, and intention generates a force that shapes the individual's future experiences. It is the belief that one's actions in the present life determine the nature of one's future existences. The concept of karma assumes that the universe operates according to a system of cause and effect, where moral actions lead to positive outcomes, and immoral actions yield negative consequences.

In the case of Jimmy Savile, his alleged malevolent actions as a sexual predator stand in stark contrast to the ostensible goodness exemplified through his charitable work. By engaging in philanthropy, Savile may have sought to counterbalance the negative energy generated by his hidden transgressions. This delicate dance between darkness and light allowed him to maintain a complex equilibrium, where his predatory acts could be veiled behind a carefully curated facade of benevolence. Thus, through his charity work, he gained a figurative path to redemption, presenting himself as a force for good and deflecting suspicion from his darker intentions.

Additionally, Savile's charity work may have served as a strategic tool to gain access to influential figures, including politicians, members of the royal family, and other individuals of power and prestige. By positioning himself at the nexus of charitable causes, Savile cleverly created opportunities to interact with the upper echelons of society. Attending charity events, fundraisers, and galas provided him with a direct line of communication and connection to those in positions of influence. He utilized these interactions to further solidify his web of control and expand his network of influential associates.

The image of a philanthropist adorned Savile with an aura of respectability, making him a magnet for public figures seeking to align themselves with charitable causes. His extensive charitable endeavors provided a platform for others to associate themselves with his supposed virtuousness, inadvertently granting him a shield of protection against scrutiny. This symbiotic relationship allowed Savile to exert influence over his high-profile connections, potentially exploiting them for his personal gain or leveraging his social capital to manipulate situations to his advantage.

Moreover, Savile's charity work offered him an opportunity to cultivate gratitude and indebtedness from those directly benefiting from his philanthropy. By bestowing favors, granting wishes, and providing support, he established an environment of reliance and gratitude among his recipients. through various acts of kindness, Savile engineered a sense of obligation that further solidified his influence over those within his charitable network. This dynamic fueled a reciprocal relationship where he held the power to exploit the vulnerabilities of those who felt beholden to him, cementing his position of control.

Furthermore, Savile's charity work facilitated a kind of social alchemy, transforming the energy generated through acts of philanthropy into access and power. The gratitude and adoration he received from beneficiaries of his charitable endeavors fueled a form of energetic currency, which he could potentially redirect to his advantage. This energetic transaction not only granted him access to influential individuals but also allowed him to exert his influence over them, manipulating situations to achieve desired outcomes or secure his interests.

By examining the underlying dynamics of Savile's charity work, we begin to unravel the complex motivations behind his philanthropic façade. It is crucial to recognize that while some individuals engage in charitable endeavors with purely altruistic intentions, others employ philanthropy as a weapon of manipulation and social engineering. In Savile's case, the intricate interplay between balancing karma, accessing powerful connections, cultivating indebtedness, and harnessing energetic currency raises significant questions about the authenticity of his philanthropy and the underlying dark motivations that propelled his actions. Join us as we wade through the murky waters of Jimmy Savile's charity work, seeking to uncover the hidden agendas that lay beneath the surface of his seemingly benevolent contributions.

Discussion on the concept of gathering "soul energy" through public persona and philanthropy

In this thought-provoking section, we delve into the concept of gathering "soul energy" and how it ties into Jimmy Savile's public persona and philanthropic efforts. As we explore this esoteric notion, we begin to untangle the intricate web of manipulation and power that Savile may have woven through his extensive engagement with the public.

At its core, the idea of soul energy postulates that every action, interaction, and emotional exchange has an energetic component that can be harnessed and utilized by individuals. This abstract energy is believed to emanate from the essence of one's being, connecting individuals on a deeper level beyond the physical realm. In the case of Jimmy Savile, we come face to face with the possibility that his charismatic public persona and extensive philanthropy were employed as tools to gather this soul energy, subsequently exploiting it for his own gain.

Consider the sheer scale of Savile's public persona – a larger-than-life figure who captured the attention and affection of millions. His television appearances, charismatic interviews, and public events painted an enchanting portrait of a beloved figure, seemingly brimming with kindness, generosity, and a genuine concern for the welfare of others. Yet, behind this carefully constructed image, there lies the potential for a calculated effort to gather the soul energy of those who fell under Savile's spell.

By skillfully interacting with the public, Savile created a symbiotic relationship where his public persona resonated deeply with individuals, evoking emotions of trust, admiration, and even adoration. Through his philanthropic endeavors, he tapped into the innate desire of humans to connect, inspire, and be inspired. This interconnectedness allowed Savile to manipulate the energetic exchanges that occurred during his interactions, potentially siphoning off the soul energy generated by those who found solace, hope, or inspiration in his seemingly virtuous actions.

Furthermore, Savile's extensive engagement with charitable causes provided him with an ample supply of individuals who collectively vested their hope, trust, and gratitude into him. As beneficiaries of his philanthropy expressed their heartfelt appreciation, their emotions infused the energetic field surrounding Savile, potentially providing him with a profound energetic source to draw upon. The energy generated by this exchange may have been perceived as a form of nourishment, empowering and uplifting him as he sought to maintain control over his victims, manipulate influential figures, or further his personal agendas.

The concept of soul energy also intersects with the notion of parasitic feeding, a concept often associated with energy vampires. These metaphoric beings are said to draw sustenance from the emotional or energetic life force of others. By actively seeking out moments of human connection, such as during public appearances or charity events, Savile may have siphoned off the vital energy of those around him. This potentially provided him with a continual source of power and influence, allowing him to further solidify his grip on unsuspecting victims or maintain sway over influential figures who unwittingly contributed to his energetic reserve.

It is important to note that the discussion of soul energy and its manipulation by Savile is speculative and based on conjecture. However, examining his interconnectedness with the public and the extent to which his public persona impacted others invites us to consider the possibility that his engagement with people operated on a deeper energetic level. This exploration sheds light on the potential mechanisms through which Savile may have wielded control, tapping into the intangible aspect of human existence and utilizing the energy generated by those who believed in his facade.

By delving into the realm of soul energy, we raise profound questions about the true intentions behind Savile's philanthropy and the depths of his manipulation. Was his charity work merely a means to gather this ethereal energy, empowering him to exert control over individuals and institutions? Did his public persona absorb the soul energy of those who admired and supported him? These queries, while abstract in nature, offer a lens through which we can examine the hidden dynamics at play within Savile's expansive web of influence, casting light on the potential ways in which he may have harnessed and manipulated the energies generated by those who unwittingly fed his power.

Chapter 10: Ley Lines and Manipulation of Subtle Forces

In this pivotal chapter, we turn our attention to a fascinating aspect of occult practices and their potential connection to Jimmy Savile. Here, we shall explore the suspected use of ley lines locations as a means of manipulating subtle forces, unveiling a hidden dimension to Savile's actions and the sites associated with his life and influence. As we navigate the intricate web of ley lines, we delve into locations such as Stoke Mandeville, Broadmoor, Duncroft, and Broadcasting House, seeking to unravel the enigmatic tapestry woven by these mysterious energy pathways.

To fully grasp the significance of ley lines, we must embark on a journey through time and space. Ley lines, conceived by Alfred Watkins in the early 20th century, are believed to be invisible lines linking ancient sites of importance, traversing the landscape like energetic veins that pulse with mystic power. These alignments, which often coincide with prehistoric landmarks, sacred sites, and religious monuments, are thought to carry potent energy, connecting disparate points on the Earth's surface.

It is within this framework that we encounter Stoke Mandeville, a place intriguingly intertwined with Jimmy Savile's life. Originally a small village nestled in the heart of Buckinghamshire, Stoke Mandeville gained notoriety as a hub for charitable work and, more significantly, as the birthplace of the Paralympic movement. Savile himself was renowned for his extensive involvement with the Stoke Mandeville Hospital, where he dedicated countless hours to helping patients and raising substantial funds. However, as we peel back the surface, questions arise regarding the true nature of his connection to Stoke Mandeville, and whether its unique energy alignment played a role in his activities.

Another focal point of our investigation is Broadmoor, Britain's most notorious high-security psychiatric hospital. Situated within the dense woodlands of Berkshire, Broadmoor has long been associated with stories of madness, violence, and the sinister underbelly of society. Savile found himself deeply embedded in the world of Broadmoor, serving as a volunteer for decades and enjoying unparalleled access to its inhabitants, some of whom were convicted of heinous crimes. Could it be mere coincidence that this infamous institution lies amidst the intersecting ley lines, potentially amplifying its own unique energetic currents?

Duncroft, a former girls' school located in Surrey, comprises another intriguing location within Savile's orbit. This institution held a dark secret, drawing the attention of investigators in recent years. Reports of abuse, manipulation, and control emerged, painting a grim picture of the underbelly of power that pervaded the walls of Duncroft. As we examine the energetic landscape in which this institution resided, we unearth disconcerting questions about Savile's potential utilization of the nearby ley lines for his own malevolent ends.

Lastly, our exploration takes us to Broadcasting House, the iconic headquarters of the British Broadcasting Corporation (BBC). As the epicenter of the British media landscape, this esteemed institution lies entrenched within the interconnected tapestry of ley lines that crisscross the United Kingdom. Savile's close association with the BBC is well-documented, where he enjoyed a storied career as a television and radio presenter. Given the potential connection between ley lines and the manipulation of subtle forces, we must question whether Broadcasting House acted as a nexus, enhancing Savile's influence over the nation through the electromagnetic currents flowing beneath the surface.

By examining these ley line locations, we aim to shed light on the possible utilization of their energetic power by Jimmy Savile. Could there be hidden occult rituals occurring within these sites, with Savile harnessing the subtle forces within the ley lines? Is it plausible that his extensive connections, influence, and actions were, to a certain extent, orchestrated through the manipulation of these ancient and potent energy lines?

In this chapter, we shall unravel the intricate relationships between Savile, ley lines, and the sites of significance in his life, contemplating the implications of these connections on his actions and motivations. By exploring the entwined mysteries of these ancient energy pathways, we inch closer to unraveling the enigma that was Jimmy Savile and the potential occult forces that underpinned his actions.

Exploration of the suspected use of ley line locations by Savile for manipulation of subtle energies

In this section of Chapter 10, we embark on a detailed exploration of the suspected use of ley line locations by Jimmy Savile, shedding light on the potential manipulation of subtle energies that might have been at play during his enigmatic life. As we delve into this intricate web of occult practices and energetic forces, we uncover the underlying mechanisms that could have facilitated Savile's control and influence over both individuals and society at large.

Ley lines, often defined as invisible alignments connecting sacred or significant sites, have fascinated occult practitioners, archaeologists, and scholars for decades. These energy pathways, believed to carry a distinct vibrational frequency, cut across landscapes, traversing mountains, rivers, and ancient monuments. By tapping into the energetic currents flowing along ley lines, magicians, mystics, and adepts throughout history sought to harness and manipulate these forces for various purposes, from ritualistic practices to personal empowerment and societal control.

Within the context of our investigation, we turn our attention to the curious interconnection between Savile and specific ley line locations that played prominent roles in his life. Stoke Mandeville, a village situated in proximity to Aylesbury, Buckinghamshire, emerges as a focal point of inquiry due to its alignment on the ley line grid. This location served as a backdrop to Savile's extensive charity work, particularly his association with the Stoke Mandeville Hospital and the endorsement of the Paralympic movement. While Savile's involvement initially appeared noble and altruistic, the potential influence wrought by the energetic currents of the ley line raises intriguing questions about the true nature of his activities.

Furthermore, we explore the enigmatic relationship between Savile and Broadmoor Hospital, nestled deep within the ancient woodlands of Crowthorne, Berkshire. This high-security psychiatric institution, home to some of Britain's most notorious individuals, operates alongside a convergence of ley lines, imbuing the site with its unique energetic signature. Savile's longstanding association with Broadmoor, as both a volunteer and a seemingly omnipresent figure, raises suspicions about the potentially malevolent forces at work. Were the ley line currents manipulated to exert control over the inmates or amplify the hidden aspect of Savile's influence within the hospital walls?

Turning our attention to Duncroft, a former girls' school located in Staines-upon-Thames, Surrey, we uncover yet another striking connection to Savile and ley lines. Reports of abuse, manipulation, and coercion within the institution have surfaced, prompting us to scrutinize the role of energetic currents flowing through the nearby ley lines. Might these subtle forces have been harnessed by Savile to enable his control and exploitation of vulnerable young girls? Was Duncroft chosen as a strategic location due to its resonance with his desired intent, amplified by the ley line energies intertwined with its grounds?

Lastly, we must examine Broadcasting House, the renowned headquarters of the British Broadcasting Corporation (BBC), and its correlation to ley lines. With Savile's prominent career as a television and radio presenter, his deep connections within the British media landscape cannot be understated. Situated within the energetic web of ley lines, Broadcasting House potentially served as a conduit for the transmission of subtle forces, enhancing Savile's influence over the nation. The electromagnetic currents underpinning the building may have acted as a vehicle for both his charismatic presence on screen and his manipulation of public perception.

Throughout this exploration, we should approach these potential connections with discernment and open-minded inquiry. The interplay between ley lines and Savile's activities invites us to contemplate and investigate whether the convergence of these energetic currents played a role in enhancing his psychological power, enabling him to surreptitiously manipulate, control, and exert influence over individuals and societal structures.

By scrutinizing the ley line locations associated with Savile's life, we begin to glimpse the potential interplay between the occult forces and the actions of this enigmatic figure. Were these ancient energy channels utilized strategically or inadvertently? Did they facilitate the subtle manipulation of energetic currents, aiding in the realization of Savile's dark intentions? In the further exploration of this chapter, we shall continue to investigate the implications of these ley line connections, endeavoring to unravel the enigmatic tapestry that surrounds Jimmy Savile's alleged occult practices and their influence on his actions and motivations.

Analysis of specific locations associated with Savile, such as Stoke Mandeville, Broadmoor, Duncroft, and Broadcasting House

In this section of Chapter 10, we undertake a comprehensive analysis of the specific locations closely associated with Jimmy Savile, delving into their potential significance and the role they played in his alleged manipulation of subtle energies. Stoke Mandeville, Broadmoor, Duncroft, and Broadcasting House emerge as key sites of interest, each intertwined with its own unique set of circumstances and energetic influences.

Stoke Mandeville, the tranquil village situated in the heart of Buckinghamshire, holds a particular fascination when examining Savile's life. Not only was it the backdrop for his extensive charity work, but it also played a pivotal role in the formation of the Paralympic movement. Savile's connection with Stoke Mandeville Hospital, where he dedicated countless hours of his time, raised substantial funds, and championed the cause of disabled individuals, appeared to be an embodiment of pure philanthropy. However, as we unravel the potential influence of ley lines in this location, questions surface about whether Savile's actions were motivated by a deeper, hidden purpose. Did the energetic currents flowing through the ley lines intersecting Stoke Mandeville contribute to his ability to captivate, manipulate, and control those around him? Could these unseen forces have fueled his insatiable thirst for power and influence?

Broadmoor Hospital, located amidst the ancient woodlands of Crowthorne, Berkshire, presents another tantalizing location in our investigation. Renowned as Britain's highest-security psychiatric institution, Broadmoor has long held a shadowy allure due to its association with some of the country's most notorious individuals. Savile's involvement with the institution, spanning several decades, and his unusual access to patients within its walls, raise unsettling questions about the potential manipulation of subtle energies. With the convergence of ley lines at Broadmoor, we hypothesize about the possible amplification of hidden influences and psychological control that facilitated Savile's pervasive presence within this institution. Were these energetic currents harnessed to perpetuate his dark agenda, granting him an uncanny ability to exert dominance over both staff and patients alike?

Duncroft, a former girls' school nestled in Staines-upon-Thames, Surrey, holds its own secrets within the context of Savile's alleged occult practices. Reports of abuse, manipulation, and coercion have emerged, painting a grim picture of the insidious undercurrents that pervaded the institution. As we explore the energetic landscape surrounding Duncroft, we speculate on whether the nearby ley lines played a role in facilitating Savile's control over vulnerable young girls. Could the convergence and intersection of these subtle energetic pathways have afforded him a far-reaching hold on the minds and emotions of his victims? Did the energetic resonance of Duncroft, facilitated by the ley lines, potentiate his manipulative powers, allowing him to exploit and subjugate those within his reach?

Lastly, our analysis brings us to Broadcasting House, the celebrated headquarters of the British Broadcasting Corporation (BBC). As the pulsating nerve center of the British media landscape, Broadcasting House assumes a critical role in understanding Savile's alleged manipulation of subtle forces. His profound presence within the BBC, spanning numerous television and radio programs, positioned him as an influential figure with unparalleled access to the public consciousness. Nested within the energetic grid of ley lines, we ponder the augmentation of his abilities to captivate and influence through the electromagnetic currents flowing beneath the edifice. Broadcasting House potentially acted as a nexus, synergizing the convergence of ley lines and amplifying the energetic transmissions broadcast by Savile. We contemplate whether this energetic alignment, consciously or unconsciously, played a role in facilitating his dominion over the thoughts, emotions, and perceptions of the nation.

By carefully scrutinizing these specific locations intimately connected to Jimmy Savile's life, we aim to unravel the intricate interplay between the energetic currents of ley lines and his alleged manipulation of subtle forces. These sites, whether by design or happenstance, appear to have converged with Savile's actions, raising thought-provoking questions about the interrelationship between space, energy, and the human psyche. As we delve deeper into our analysis, we endeavor to shed light on the complex web of occult influences that may have afforded Savile the means to exert control, achieve dominance, and satisfy his insatiable hunger for power and influence.

Discussion on the potential impact of ley lines in occult practices and personal/societal control

In this captivating section of Chapter 10, we enter the realm of speculative exploration, delving into the potential impact of ley lines in occult practices and their ability to facilitate personal and societal control. As we contemplate the energetic resonances of Stoke Mandeville, Broadmoor, Duncroft, and Broadcasting House, we unravel the intricate tapestry of hidden forces that might have played a role in Jimmy Savile's alleged manipulation and influence.

To comprehend the potential impact of ley lines in occult practices, we must first understand the esoteric concept of subtle energies that permeate the cosmic fabric and intersect with our physical reality. In many ancient spiritual and occult traditions, it is believed that space is imbued with a web of interconnected forces, often referred to as aetheric or astral energies. Within this framework, ley lines are seen as channels through which this subtle energy flows, forming a network that crisscrosses the Earth's surface. These energy lines, when intersecting sacred or significant sites, are thought to amplify the potency of any practices conducted within their vicinity.

The occultist views ley lines as conduits for harnessing and directing the mystical forces that underlie the universe. By tapping into these energetic currents, practitioners seek to manipulate and control subtle energies for a variety of purposes, ranging from personal spiritual advancement to the exertion of psychological dominance over others. These practices often involve rituals, spells, or other intentional acts that resonate with the energy currents flowing along ley lines.

Considering the potential influence of ley lines on personal and societal control, it is imperative to examine the locations closely associated with Savile's life and actions. Stoke Mandeville, with its alignment on the ley line grid, becomes a focal point for such contemplation. A convergence of subtle forces in this location may have created an energetic backdrop that heightened Savile's abilities to captivate and manipulate others. Through the interplay of his charismatic presence and the resonances of Stoke Mandeville's ley lines, Savile's capacity to exert psychological power and influence may well have been amplified. This raises intriguing questions as to whether his extensive charity work and the level of adoration he received were modulated by these unseen forces, aiding in the cultivation of a public image designed to deceive and control.

Broadmoor Hospital, shrouded in its own dark mystique and energetic intersections, offers another arena for examination. As one of the most infamous psychiatric institutions in the United Kingdom, Broadmoor has become synonymous with madness and the shadowy aspects of the human psyche. Within such an environment, the presence of ley lines potentially imparted an intensified energetic landscape, enabling Savile to exert further control over both inmates and staff. If Savile were consciously or unconsciously attuned to these ley line currents, then the energy flowing through Broadmoor may have facilitated his ability to manipulate and dominate those within its confines. This consideration unveils a sinister presence lurking behind the facade of his charitable involvement, suggesting an intricate dance of subtle forces and malevolent intent.

Duncroft, a once-dormant institution now notorious for its reports of abuse, manipulation, and coercion, provides yet another layer of inquiry into the potential impact of ley lines on personal and societal control. With the convergence of ley lines in the vicinity, we contemplate whether the subtle energetic currents potentiated Savile's powers of manipulation over vulnerable young girls. It is conceivable that the combination of psychological influence, facilitated by his charismatic persona, and the resonant energy of the surrounding ley lines created an atmosphere that rendered the victims more susceptible to his control. The insidious interplay between unseen forces and human vulnerability could have paved the way for Savile's systematic exploitation and abuse.

Lastly, we turn to Broadcasting House, the epicenter of the British media landscape and the site of Savile's prolific career as a television and radio personality. Nestled within the energetic grid of ley lines, this institution becomes a focal point for considering the societal control potentially facilitated by subtle energy currents. Broadcasting House served as the gateway through which Savile disseminated his captivating presence and charismatic influence to the nation. With the convergence of ley lines at this hub of communication, it is conceivable that the energetic currents acted as conduits, amplifying his ability to sway public opinion, shape collective consciousness, and maintain a dominant presence within the media landscape. The unseen energetic forces, synergized with his manipulative agenda, may have played a role in cementing his psychological grip over the minds of the public.

As we navigate the enigmatic relationship between ley lines and personal/societal control, it is crucial to approach this speculation with discernment and intellectual curiosity. While the potential impact of energetic currents flowing along ley lines should not be dismissed, definitive proof of their influence on human behavior remains elusive. However, the interplay between unseen forces and the intricate web of Jimmy Savile's life and actions offers a compelling framework through which to contemplate the possible convergence of occult practices, ley lines, and personal/societal control. The exploration of this nexus challenges us to push the boundaries of understanding, questioning established narratives, and innovatively considering the interrelationship between esoteric forces and the human experience.

Chapter 11: Unravelling the Mystery

In this captivating chapter, we delve deep into the heart of the mystery surrounding Jimmy Savile, seeking to unveil the truth behind his alleged power, motivations, and the extent of his influence. As we navigate the labyrinthine twists and turns of his life, we encounter a myriad of unanswered questions and uncertainties that challenge our understanding of this enigmatic figure.

One of the most perplexing aspects of Savile's life lies in the ambiguity surrounding his backstory. Despite his prominent position in British society, there remains a veil of secrecy shrouding his early years. Born into a working-class family in Leeds, little is known about the circumstances of his upbringing and the events that moulded the man he would become. Some speculate that this dearth of information is not merely coincidental but rather a deliberate obfuscation, hinting at a potentially hidden agenda or a role far more clandestine than initially apparent.

Rumours persist concerning Savile's possible involvement in covert operations during the war. Some suggest he may have acted as a secret spy or a "fixer," utilising his charisma and connections to navigate the shadows of an uncertain world. This theory gains further traction when we consider the historical association between secret services, intelligence agencies, and the realms of the occult. Throughout history, various covert operatives have been linked to clandestine societies and practices that harness mystical forces for their own ends. Consequently, we are left to ponder the extent to which Savile may have been entwined with such mysterious endeavours.

Compounding the intrigue is his unquestionably close association with prominent figures in British society, including members of the royal family and the political elite. This nexus of influence raises the spectre of secret society affiliations and the potential manipulation of occult forces that lie hidden in the annals of history. Savile's connections and influence extended beyond the entertainment industry, positioning him as a powerful intermediary between various spheres of power.

Such associations have long been emblematic of the symbiotic relationship between secret societies and royals. From the historical connections of the Freemasons to the aristocracy to the rumoured occult practices of various monarchies, the enigmatic ties between those in power and the esoteric arts are intertwined throughout time. This begs the question: Was Jimmy Savile's rise to prominence and the extent of his influence a product of these hidden allegiances, engendering a hidden narrative that transcends mere entertainment and seamlessly melds with a darker occult agenda?

Furthermore, we are led down the intricate maze of dualistic magic, fraught with shades of both black and white, good and evil. Savile's actions, motivations, and the consequences of his influence raise questions regarding the ethereal spectrum of magic, where intentions and outcomes are never as clear-cut as they may seem. Could it be that Savile possessed the ability to tap into both benevolent and malevolent forces, manipulating the metaphysical fabric of reality for his own ends? The ensuing exploration forces us to grapple with the complexities of morality, accountability, and the elusive nature of truth.

As we traverse the untrodden paths of Savile's life, we cannot escape the alluring allure of his charitable work, which had garnered immense admiration and accolades. Yet, beneath the surface of these noble endeavours, we question whether there existed ulterior motives lurking, like hidden serpents beneath a beguiling smile. Was his charity work a mere façade to balance the scales of karma, or did it provide a conduit for channelling the energy of thousands, perhaps even acting as a potent source for Savile's own ambitions? The links between philanthropy, celebrity status, and the manipulation of "soul energy" emerge as we contemplate the deeper purpose behind Savile's public persona.

Perhaps most intriguing of all is the speculation surrounding Savile's potential utilisation of ley lines, powerful energetic pathways that traverse the Earth's surface. These ancient and arcane conduits are believed to carry subtle forces, serving as conduits for both spiritual and magical energies. Stoke Mandeville, Broadmoor, Duncroft, and Broadcasting House—all of these locations associated with Savile's life and influence—align with the intricate web of ley lines that crisscross the British Isles. Observing this convergence of places of power, we cannot help but wonder at Savile's potential manipulation of these subtle forces for his own benefit and control.

In conclusion, this chapter delves into the vast web of mysteries surrounding Jimmy Savile, unveiling the complexities and ambiguities that taint his legacy. From the uncertainty surrounding his early years and potential involvement in covert operations to his associations with the influential elite and the tantalising connections to secret societies and the occult, Savile's life becomes a captivating enigma. Additionally, we confront the moral quandaries posed by dualistic magic and question his philanthropic endeavours as a mere facade for deeper manipulations. Lastly, we explore the convergence of ley lines and their potential role in Savile's personal and societal control. It is within these interwoven narratives that the true essence of Jimmy Savile's enigmatic existence is unveiled, leaving us with more questions than answers.

Questions surrounding Jimmy Savile's alleged power, motivations, and the expanse of his influence

As we venture deeper into the intricate tapestry of Jimmy Savile's life, the questions surrounding his alleged power, motivations, and the vastness of his influence demand our attention. What drove this enigmatic figure to pursue his insidious agenda? How did he acquire such control and command over others? And just how far-reaching were the tendrils of his influence within British society and beyond?

To explore these questions, we must first acknowledge the sheer audacity of Savile's actions. The extent of his offenses, spanning decades and encompassing hundreds of victims, suggests a level of power and manipulation far beyond the comprehension of ordinary individuals. What fueled this insatiable appetite for control and domination? And what drove him to employ the cloak of respectability to ensure his actions remained veiled from public scrutiny?

Some have posited that Savile's motivations may have been rooted in a desire for self-gratification and the pursuit of untamed desires. Yet, as we peel back the layers of his life, we encounter the unnerving possibility that his motivations extended beyond mere personal satisfaction. Could it be that Savile was tapping into a wellspring of hidden knowledge, a more profound understanding of occult practices and esoteric arts? Were his actions guided by a quest for power, fueled by an understanding of ancient rituals and their potential to manipulate the energetic fabric of reality?

One cannot help but draw parallels between Savile and the archetype of the "energy vampire," those individuals who feed upon the life-force of others to sustain their own vitality. Count Dracula himself, a figure of folklore and literature, possesses this characteristic, tapping into the awe and admiration of his victims to sustain his immortal existence. In a similar vein, Savile seemed to possess an uncanny ability to gather energy, not through ghoulish means, but through his carefully curated public image and extensive philanthropic endeavors.

His philanthropy, initially seen as virtuous, takes on a more sinister hue when viewed through the lens of occult practices. Savile's charitable work, built upon the backs of countless donors, could potentially have served as a means to amass a steady supply of what can only be described as "soul energy." The goodwill and positive intentions of those who believed in his benevolence could have unknowingly fueled the hidden rituals and hidden agendas lurking beneath the veneer of generosity. But to what end? Did Savile harness this energy to augment his own power, manipulate the fates of those within his sphere, or perhaps to further catalyze his connection to the occult forces that purportedly guided his actions?

Furthermore, we must confront the alarming possibility that Savile was not acting alone. His extensive network of connections, ranging from royalty to politicians and influential figures of all walks of life, hints at a far more pervasive presence of dark influence within British society. Could Savile have served as a mere pawn in a larger game, manipulated by hidden hands operating in the shadows? Or was he a willing agent, leveraging his position and charisma to further an agenda shrouded in secrecy and woven with threads of occult power?

The convergence of Savile's life with the world of secret societies and their associated symbolism is also worth examining. Throughout history, secret societies have thrived on the esoteric knowledge and rituals they guard, manipulating societal narratives and exerting control over individuals in positions of power. Symbols play a crucial role in their practices, harnessing archetypes, and evoking subtle energetic influences. As we consider Savile's presence within this intricate tapestry, we must analyze the symbols he employed, the hidden meanings behind his actions, and his potential alignment with the tenets of these age-old clandestine organizations.

Ultimately, our quest to understand the depth of Savile's power, motivations, and influence leads us to question the very fabric of reality and the hidden forces that shape our world. Was he a master manipulator, expertly navigating the currents of power and control? Were his actions driven by a malevolent agency hell-bent on harnessing occult energies for darker purposes? Or could there be an even more profound explanation, one that pushes the boundaries of our understanding and veers into the realm of the supernatural?

As we journey further into the depths of Savile's life, we must prepare ourselves for the unsettling truths that may lay in wait. In the murky depths of this investigation, we seek to uncover the motivations behind his actions, to unravel the enigma of his influence, and to challenge our perceptions of reality. The answers to these probing questions lie somewhere within the shadows, awaiting discovery and revelation, as we seek to shine a light on the dark arts of Jimmy Savile.

Examination of the uncertainty surrounding his backstory and potential secret spy or "fixer" role during the war

An aspect that adds to the mystique and intrigue of Jimmy Savile is the uncertainty that shrouds his backstory, particularly his early years and the events that shaped his enigmatic persona. Born into a working-class family in Leeds on October 31, 1926, Savile's journey from his humble beginnings to becoming a household name raises questions about the hidden layers of his life and potential involvement in covert operations.

Speculation abounds regarding Savile's possible role as a secret spy or a "fixer" during the war. Many notable figures of the time were enlisted to serve in secretive capacities, their talents and connections exploited to further the interests of their nations. Given Savile's charismatic nature, his connections within the entertainment industry, and his growing influence, it isn't entirely far-fetched to consider the possibility that he may have operated in the shadows during this tumultuous period.

While concrete evidence to substantiate these claims remains elusive, researchers and theorists have examined several pieces of the puzzle that hint at a more clandestine aspect to Savile's life. His acquaintance with powerful individuals and connections to secret societies evoke the notion that his rise to prominence may have been orchestrated rather than a simple stroke of luck. It raises the question: Was his ascent a calculated maneuver, designed to position him in a role that blended seamlessly into the fabric of society while simultaneously serving hidden interests?

Such theories gain further weight when we consider the historical alignment between intelligence agencies, covert operations, and the enigmatic realm of the occult. Throughout history, those involved in the clandestine arts have been known to harness arcane knowledge, hidden symbols, and esoteric practices to maintain control over unsuspecting populations. Instances of influential individuals operating within these interconnected domains are not without precedent, as the allure of magic and the occult has often found fertile ground within the intelligence community.

The notion of occult practices and their potential alignment with covert operations can be traced back to a web of connections that extend into the foggy realms of history. The ancient art of espionage has long drawn inspiration from the mystical and occult. From the utilization of symbolism and coded languages to harnessing the energies of hidden knowledge, spies have sought to manipulate events and individuals by tapping into the unseen forces that govern our world.

Savile's magnetic persona, innate charm, and propensity for manipulating others hint at a deeper well of knowledge and skill. Was he, perhaps, a master of psychological manipulation, employing a combination of charm, coercion, and esoteric techniques to bend individuals to his will? Was his influence over the powerful figures of his time a product of skillful puppetry that allowed him to sway the course of events for his own benefit? These questions illuminate the tantalizing connections that lie between Savile's rise to prominence, the shadowy world of secret operations, and the occult practices that may have fueled his ascent.

Throughout history, individuals who have operated in the shadows have often possessed a duality of purpose and persona. The public image they project may be a cleverly crafted facade, obscuring their true role as agents of influence and manipulation. Savile's ability to seamlessly transition between the realms of entertainment and public service raises the possibility of a complicated life lived between the spotlight and the shadows, where he navigated the desires of the powerful and the hidden machinations of those who sought to control the world.

As we attempt to unravel the mysteries surrounding Savile's potential involvement as a secret spy or a "fixer" during the war, we find ourselves venturing into the realms of speculation, where fragments of evidence and conjecture punctuate the enigmatic tapestry that was his life. The intertwined nature of covert operations and occult practices opens a Pandora's box of possibilities, suggesting that Jimmy Savile's true role and motivations may have extended far beyond the realm of public celebrity. Only by continuing our exploration can we hope to peel back the layers of this complex enigma and shed light on the truth that lies hidden within the shadows.

Analysis of the known connections between secret services, occult practices, and influential figures

As we plunge deeper into the labyrinth of Jimmy Savile's life, we encounter a web of connections that intertwines secret services, occult practices, and influential figures. To comprehend the extent of Savile's power and influence, we must explore the historical associations between hidden agendas, esoteric knowledge, and the mysterious realms of the occult.

Throughout history, secret services and intelligence organizations have operated hand in hand with the enigmatic arts. The convergence of knowledge and power between these clandestine agencies and the occult has birthed a realm where hidden hands manipulate events, individuals, and the very fabric of society. Savile's alleged involvement with secret societies, coupled with his charismatic persona and connections to influential figures, raises the specter of his potential engagement in covert operations that veiled a deeper occult agenda.

One of the most notorious secret societies associated with the occult is the Freemasons, an ancient and influential fraternity with a history deeply intertwined with symbolism, ritual practices, and the pursuit of hidden knowledge. Freemasonry has often been linked to political influence, positions of power, and connections between influential individuals. Within this esoteric brotherhood lie degrees that explore mystical aspects of reality and seek to reveal hidden truths. Though concrete evidence tying Savile to Freemasonry remains elusive, speculation regarding his possible membership arises from his connections within the British establishment, his honors and knighthoods, and his public persona of wielding clandestine influence.

Another secret society connected to occult practices is the Ordo Templi Orientis (OTO), founded by the notorious occultist Aleister Crowley. Crowley, known as "The Great Beast" and a master of occult arts, delved into the realms of ceremonial magic, the Kabbalah, and secret initiation rituals. It is intriguing to note the parallels between Crowley's beliefs and practices and alleged connections to Thelema religion – in which Savile is also believed to be involved – suggesting the possibility of a shared fascination with hidden knowledge and esoteric practices. These connections open the door to speculation about Savile's potential apprenticeship under a darker mentor steeped in the mysteries of the occult.

The historical affiliation between intelligence agencies and the occult, though often clouded in secrecy, is a well-known undercurrent. During times of global conflict, clandestine organizations have sought every advantage, often employing unorthodox methods to gain insights and control. Techniques such as remote viewing, psychic phenomena, and manipulation of subtle energies have been explored to gain the upper hand. These covert efforts have frequently crossed paths with occult circles, where practitioners claim access to supernatural knowledge and the manipulation of hidden forces. The notion that Savile's alleged involvement in secret operations intersects with these realms of hidden knowledge adds another layer to the tapestry of his mysterious life.

When examining influential figures associated with the occult, it is crucial to acknowledge their historical connections with the British monarchy. Throughout the centuries, British royals have shown an enduring fascination with hidden knowledge, secret societies, and mystical practices. From the alleged practices of John Dee, the Elizabethan court magician, to the enigmatic pursuits of Prince Charles, the connections between the occult and British royalty cannot be easily dismissed. The ambiguous gift of cigars and a note from Prince Charles to Savile further fuels speculation about a shared understanding or connection between the two men, hinting at deeper connections obscured from public view.

These historical associations between secret services, occult practices, and influential figures may provide a framework within which we can understand the enigma that is Jimmy Savile. They hint at a deeper layer of influence and control manipulated by those who walk the tightrope between power, knowledge, and the hidden forces that shape our world. As we contemplate the connections between Savile and these realms, we must question whether his rise to prominence and the vastness of his influence were a product of these hidden connections, a symbiotic dance between the occult and the intelligence community, orchestrated to serve hidden interests.

In conclusion, the known connections between secret services, occult practices, and influential figures offer us a glimpse into the complexities of Jimmy Savile's life. The historical associations between espionage, hidden knowledge, and societal control point to a shadowy web that might have entangled Savile's actions and motivations. As we navigate the serpentine paths of secret societies and explore the enigmatic realms of the occult, we inch closer to unraveling the truths that lie hidden within the depths of his story. The hidden hands that shape our world may reveal themselves, granting us a glimpse into the sinister machinations that remain untold beneath the surface of Jimmy Savile's infamous legacy.

Chapter 12: Conclusion

As our journey through the dark arts of Jimmy Savile nears its conclusion, we stand on the precipice of a formidable array of theories and connections that challenge our perceptions of the man once revered as a national treasure. In this final chapter, we gather the strands of our exploration, weaving them together to bring us closer to unmasking the occult secrets hidden within Savile's enigmatic life.

Throughout this captivating investigation, we have scrutinized the intricate web of influence, connections, and alleged occult practices that surrounded Savile. We have examined his associations with influential figures from various fields, exposing the potentially sinister motivations behind his wide-ranging network. From politicians to royalty, from musicians to prominent television personalities, Savile skillfully maneuvered in circles where power and influence collided, raising alarming questions about the depths of his network and the true nature of his partnerships.

Moreover, we have unearthed the significance of Savile's honors and knighthoods, bestowing upon him the titles of a Knight of Malta, a Knight Commander of St. Gregory, and a Knight of the Realm. Such prestigious accolades, often intertwined with occult connotations and connections to hidden societies, hint at an individual vested in secretive agendas and clandestine practices that supersede the public persona he projected.

The analysis of Savile's language and symbols has allowed us to pierce through the veil of his carefully constructed persona, highlighting the use of phrases like "jingle jangle," which may have held hidden meanings comprehensible only to those initiated in occult practices. By understanding the ancient and esoteric power of language and symbols, we have exposed the manipulative tactics that Savile may have employed to exert control and mesmerize those he encountered.

Our exploration has revealed striking parallels between Savile and the notorious English occultist, Alastair Crowley. Both were enigmatic figures associated with the Thelema religion and the use of occult symbols. Moreover, we have traced the peculiar influence of Thelema on the music scene of the 1960s, particularly the pervasive impact on iconic bands like The Beatles, ultimately leading us to question the extent of Savile's occult infiltration within the realms of popular culture.

By traversing Savile's charitable work, we have uncovered a potentially chilling ulterior motive behind his philanthropic endeavors. Our investigation has suggested that his charity work served as a means to balance karma, to gain access to influential figures, and, disconcertingly, to gather what can only be described as "soul energy." Through his public persona and charitable exploits, Savile may have harnessed the energy generated by the admiration and reverence of others to fuel his own hidden agenda.

The manipulation of subtle forces through the utilization of ley line locations has been another intriguing aspect of our exploration. By examining specific locations associated with Savile, such as Stoke Mandeville, Broadmoor, Duncroft, and Broadcasting House, we have raised questions about the potential manipulation of mystical forces, further blurring the line between the mundane and the occult.

Throughout this journey, we have pondered the intriguing comparison between Savile and the legendary Count Dracula, both portrayed as energy vampires, exploiting the life force of those around them. This comparison amplifies our understanding of the occult undercurrents that may have fueled Savile's actions, wherein he sought not only physical gratification but potentially harnessed an unseen energy to empower himself.

The examination of Savile's potential duality in the practice of magic, encompassing both black and white magic, has added complexity to his persona. This duality offers insight into the motivations behind his actions and brings to light the blurred line between good and evil, where manipulation, control, and personal gain intermingle.

Throughout the course of our investigation, we have encountered tantalizing hints of secret society affiliations, connections with royalty, and the obscure world of intelligence agencies. The potential intertwining of these forces, combined with the history of occult practices within influential circles, affords a broader context for understanding Savile's actions and motivations.

As we draw this exploration to a close, it is important to acknowledge the vast uncertainties that remain surrounding Savile's backstory, potentially casting him as a secret spy or "fixer" during the war. The possibilities of his involvement in covert activities, coupled with the known associations between secret services, occult practices, and influential figures, create an unsettling backdrop for understanding the enigma that was Jimmy Savile.

In concluding our meticulous examination, we are left grappling with profound questions. What were the true intentions behind Savile's actions? How extensive was his nefarious influence? Did he exploit the occult forces surrounding him to manipulate and control those within his reach? The answers to these questions may forever elude us, but the unveiling of the occult secrets hidden beneath his public image sparks an urgent call for further research and investigation to shed light on the untold depths of his involvement in the darker realms of esoteric knowledge.

As we bring this chapter, and indeed our entire exploration, to a close, we are left with a chilling reminder that the truth often lies veiled beneath the surface, awaiting the curious and the persistent to unravel its mysteries. The dark arts of Jimmy Savile have laid bare a convoluted web of occult connections and potentially sinister undertakings, serving as a poignant reminder that beneath the outward veneer of fame and goodwill, a darker and more treacherous reality may lurk.

Summary of the Various Theories and Connections Explored

As we reach the penultimate section of our investigation into the dark arts of Jimmy Savile, we must pause and reflect on the vast array of theories and connections we have explored throughout this journey. Each revelation and inquiry has brought us closer to unraveling the hidden occult secrets that lie beneath the surface of Savile's public image. Let us now recapitulate the key elements and theories that have shaped our understanding thus far.

The web of connections that Savile wove throughout his life is a central theme that permeates our investigation. From politicians to royalty, from entertainers to influential figures in various sectors, Savile's ability to forge relationships with individuals from all walks of life is remarkable and raises unsettling questions. As we have discovered, these connections extend far beyond the realm of mere association, hinting at a hidden influence and potentially shared occult practices among these individuals.

Furthermore, we have delved into the significance of Savile's prestigious honors and knighthoods, such as the Knight of Malta, Knight Commander of St. Gregory, and Knight of the Realm. These titles possess a deep symbolism and carry with them potential implications of secret society affiliations and involvement in practices beyond the public eye. These connections shine a light on the entangled relationship between power, influence, and hidden agendas that may have influenced Savile's actions.

Language and symbolism have emerged as crucial elements in our exploration. Savile cleverly employed phrases such as "jingle jangle," whose true meaning may be concealed, accessible only to initiates in occult practices. The power of repetition and the careful selection and utilization of symbols have showcased Savile's ability to manipulate those around him, utilizing hidden cues to exert control and captivate his victims.

Drawing parallels between Savile and the notorious occultist Alastair Crowley has added another layer of intrigue to this investigation. Both have their alleged connections to Thelema, a religion emphasizing individual will and esoteric practices. The impact of Thelema on the 1960s music scene, particularly the influence on renowned bands like The Beatles, highlights the potential occult infiltration within popular culture and raises questions about Savile's role in this phenomenon.

Furthermore, we have examined Savile's extensive charitable work and the potential darker motives behind his philanthropic endeavors. Beyond their outwardly positive image, these acts of generosity may have served as a means for Savile to balance karma, gain access to influential individuals, and even harvest a form of metaphysical energy often referred to as "soul energy." Such manipulation of public perception adds a chilling depth to our understanding of Savile's actions.

The manipulation of subtle forces through ley lines has been another intriguing aspect of our exploration. By analyzing specific locations associated with Savile, we have uncovered potential links to the manipulation and harnessing of these mystical forces. The utilization of ley lines in occult practices, while often shrouded in secrecy, suggests a connection to the manipulation of energy and a deeper understanding of the unseen forces at play in Savile's actions.

In our comparison to the legendary Count Dracula, we have unraveled the concept of Savile as an energy vampire. This metaphor offers insight into the potential unseen forces that drove his actions. By tapping into the life force of those around him, Savile may have bolstered his power and influence, leaving a trail of victims in his quest for energy and control.

Unraveling the mysteries surrounding Savile's backstory has proved to be a complex challenge. As fragments of his potential involvement in covert activities and intelligence agencies emerge, we are left to question his role and potential influence beyond the realm of the known. These uncertainties, intertwined with historical connections between secret services, occult practices, and influential figures, paint a picture of a man whose life orbits around secrecy and hidden motivations.

As we draw closer to the conclusion of this investigation, the implications of our findings become increasingly weighty. The theories and connections explored throughout our exploration have illuminated a complex tapestry of occult influence, manipulation, and hidden motivations behind Savile's actions. Yet, despite our research, many questions remain unanswered, leaving ample room for further exploration, research, and investigation into the occult aspects that shaped Savile's life.

In conclusion, this comprehensive overview of the various theories and connections explored throughout our investigation serves to underscore the profound implications of unmasking Savile's occult secrets. Beyond the realm of public adoration, a multifaceted figure emerges, steeped in enigmatic affiliations, hidden symbols, and potential involvement in practices that transcend the boundaries of the conventional. The curtain is drawn back, revealing the potential darker side to Jimmy Savile's public image, leaving us to grapple with the unsettling reality that, beneath charm and generosity, lies a complex individual whose actions and motivations extend into the realm of the occult.

Final Thoughts and Suggestions for Further Exploration

As we draw our investigation into the dark arts of Jimmy Savile to a close, it is imperative to reflect on the multitude of profound and unsettling revelations that have come to light throughout our exploration. The occult secrets that lie hidden beneath Savile's public facade have shattered the illusion of a national treasure, unraveling a complex web of connections and practices that challenge our understanding of his motivations and the extent of his influence. In this final section, we offer our final thoughts and suggest avenues for continued research and exploration into this enigmatic figure.

Throughout our inquiry, we have encountered a plethora of theories and connections that hint at Savile's involvement in occult practices. The web of connections he wove with influential figures from various fields, his affiliations with prestigious organizations, and the symbolism embedded within his language and actions all point to a deeper layer of existence beyond the public's gaze. While each piece of evidence taken individually may appear circumstantial, the collective weight of these findings raises compelling questions about Savile's true nature and motivations.

Although our exploration has provided significant insights, it is crucial to acknowledge the limitations of our understanding. The questions surrounding Savile's backstory, such as his potential involvement as a secret spy or "fixer" during the war, remain tantalizingly unanswered. The ambiguous gifts and notes bestowed upon him by Prince Charles further deepen the mystery, suggesting potential connections to hidden realms of power and influence. These unresolved threads leave ample room for further investigation, urging researchers to delve deeper into the enigma that is Jimmy Savile.

To illuminate the obscure paths we have journeyed through, further examination of secret societies is essential. Uncovering potential connections between Savile and these clandestine organizations may provide critical insights into the nature of his occult ties and the extent of his influence within these networks. Exploring known connections between secret services, occult practices, and influential figures throughout history can also lay a foundation for understanding the broader context in which Savile operated.

Additionally, the analysis of the ancient and occult power of language warrants further exploration. The symbolism embedded within Savile's phrases, such as his frequent use of "jingle jangle," may hold greater significance than meets the eye. By investigating the esoteric meaning of these phrases and their potential connection to hidden rituals and practices, we may gain a deeper understanding of the extent to which his language was utilized as an instrument of manipulation and control.

Furthermore, the influence of Thelema on Savile's life and its impact on the music industry, particularly within the realms of popular culture, demands continued examination. By expanding upon our exploration of the connections between Savile and Alastair Crowley, along with the shared fascination with Thelema, researchers may unearth further evidence of occult influences permeating both Savile's life and the broader cultural landscape of his era.

Continuing our investigation into Savile's philanthropic endeavors is of paramount importance as well. Unveiling the motivations and potential hidden agendas behind his extensive charitable work can shed light on the extent to which he utilized philanthropy as a facade to gather power, influence, and perhaps even metaphysical energy. Further study could encompass the analysis of Savile's charity organizations, the connection between his chosen causes and any occult symbolism embedded within them, and the examination of possible covert manipulations through these charitable acts.

Moreover, a deeper exploration of ley lines and their potential manipulation by Savile is necessary to unveil the elusive forces that lay at the core of his alleged occult practices. Investigating the specific locations associated with him, such as Stoke Mandeville, Broadmoor, Duncroft, and Broadcasting House, in the context of ley line alignment and the occult significance of these places, may reveal deeper connections that have yet to be fully understood. Understanding the manipulation of these subtle forces could shed light on the mechanisms through which Savile purportedly harnessed metaphysical energies for his own purposes.

In conclusion, our investigation into the dark arts of Jimmy Savile has undeniably unveiled a complex web of potential occult connections, hidden practices, and motivations that defy conventional understanding. Savile's rise to fame, his extensive network of influential acquaintances, the symbolism embedded within his language and actions, and the implications of his charitable work all contribute to a portrait of a man who may have utilized the occult to exert influence and control. As we conclude this exploration, we implore future researchers to undertake further study, unravelling the enigma that is Jimmy Savile, in order to shed light on the darkest corners of his life and the true extent of his involvement in esoteric practices. It is through tireless exploration and dedication to uncovering the truth that we may come closer to understanding the intricate tapestry of occult secrets that defined his enigmatic existence.

Suggestion for Further Research and Investigation

As we bring our investigation into the dark arts of Jimmy Savile to a close, we are acutely aware that our exploration has merely scratched the surface of this fascinating and complex topic. The occult secrets that unfurled before us have opened doors to uncharted realms that beg for further research and investigation. In this final section, we propose directions for future exploration, urging scholars and truth-seekers to continue unraveling the mysteries that surround Jimmy Savile.

First and foremost, the investigation into Savile's backstory calls for in-depth examination. The lingering uncertainties surrounding his potential involvement as a secret spy or "fixer" during the war is a critical avenue for future research. Delving into historical archives, intelligence agency records, and documents related to wartime espionage may yield valuable insights into Savile's possible covert activities, shedding light on his connections, motivations, and the extent of his involvement in secretive operations.

Expanding the analysis of secret societies is another crucial area for further exploration. In order to comprehend the depths of Savile's occult ties and influence, researchers should delve into known occult societies, secret orders, and fraternal organizations. Investigating potential connections and affiliations between Savile and these clandestine groups may offer a glimpse into the occult practices and networks that shaped his actions.

The examination of Savile's connections with influential figures, such as politicians, royalty, and prominent entertainers, warrants additional scrutiny. Conducting in-depth interviews and archival research to expose any potential connections, shared interests, or overlapping agendas could unveil deeper links between Savile and these individuals. By shedding light on the hidden networks that facilitated his rise to power, researchers may further uncover the extent of his influence and the occult ties that permeated his associations.

Furthermore, further exploration into the significance of Savile's honors and knighthoods invites expansive research. Investigating the criteria and selection processes surrounding these honors, particularly those bestowed by secret societies or religious institutions, may offer additional insight into the occult dimensions of his life. Unraveling the symbolism embedded within these titles and the potential secret rituals associated with them could deepen our understanding of Savile's involvement in occult practices.

The study of occult symbolism and language in relation to Savile's actions requires continued investigation. Analyzing the hidden meanings within his phrases, gestures, and interactions may expose further connections to esoteric knowledge and rituals. By investigating the historical context and sources behind these symbols, researchers can trace the origins and potential influences that guided Savile's manipulation of language for occult purposes.

The examination of ley lines and their potential manipulation presents an intriguing avenue for future research. Mapping out additional locations associated with Savile and analyzing their alignment with ley lines can provide a more comprehensive understanding of his alleged utilization of these mysterious energy pathways. By delving into the esoteric theories surrounding ley lines and their potential ties to occult practices, researchers can shed light on the interplay between subtle forces and Savile's actions.

Lastly, broadening the research to explore the impact of occult influences in the broader cultural and social context of Savile's era is essential. Investigating the connections between occultism and the music industry, entertainment, politics, and even intelligence agencies during that time may offer a holistic understanding of the occult forces at play within society. By comprehending the broader historical and cultural context, researchers can gain a deeper appreciation of Savile's potential role in the larger occult tapestry.

In conclusion, the dark arts of Jimmy Savile have led us down a labyrinthine path infused with occult intrigue, symbolism, and hidden connections. As we part ways with this investigation, we encourage future researchers to embark on their own quests for truth, diving deeper into the enigma of Savile's life and the occult forces that shaped his actions. The journey awaits, calling for relentless curiosity, meticulous research, and an unyielding dedication to unmasking the occult secrets that shroud this notorious figure. May our collective efforts shed light on the shadowy corners of Jimmy Savile's existence, leaving no stone unturned on our quest for knowledge and truth.

Printed in Great Britain
by Amazon